Audition Speeches for Black, South Asian and Middle Eastern Actors
Monologues for Men

Audition Speeches for Black, South Asian and Middle Eastern Actors
Monologues for Men

Edited by

SIMEILIA HODGE-DALLAWAY

Bloomsbury Methuen Drama
An imprint of Bloomsbury Publishing Plc

B L O O M S B U R Y

LONDON · OXFORD · NEW YORK · NEW DELHI · SYDNEY

Bloomsbury Methuen Drama

An imprint of Bloomsbury Publishing Plc

Imprint previously known as Methuen Drama

50 Bedford Square	1385 Broadway
London	New York
WC1B 3DP	NY 10018
UK	USA

www.bloomsbury.com

BLOOMSBURY, METHUEN DRAMA and the Diana logo are trademarks of Bloomsbury Publishing Plc

First published 2016

British Library Cataloguing-in-Publication Data
A catalogue record for this book is available from the British Library

ISBN:	PB:	978-1-4742-2913-5
	ePDF:	978-1-4742-2914-2
	ePub:	978-1-4742-2915-9

Library of Congress Cataloging-in-Publication Data
A catalog record for this book is available from the Library of Congress

Cover design by Clare Turner

Typeset by Fakenham Prepress Solutions, Fakenham, Norfolk NR21 8NN
Printed and bound in Great Britain

We gratefully acknowledge financial assistance from the
Arts Council England and the National Lottery

This book is dedicated to my mother Charmaine Miller, sister Naomi Dallaway, cousin Cherene Miller and partner Reginald Edmund.

Rest in Eternal Peace
Uncle Jeremiah, Nanny Catherine and Junior Bertie

Contents

Foreword

For an actor it all begins with the word. The principal tool in an arsenal designed to assist and transmit the yearnings germinating deep within the consciousness of the writer. But much like the playwright, the actor cannot live by word alone. We playwrights are painfully aware that ours is an incomplete art form. That we need that word to be made manifest in the body, mouth and probably most importantly, the consciousness of the interpreter. These tools allow them to explore the relationship between the spoken and the spatial. To understand why the word in the first place must to be spoken rather than just read.

If any of the above is true then my next question would be to ask how do we assist the training of our translators? How do we help hone the equipment we all rely upon so badly?

My first answer would be a book such as this.

Allow me to take a step back. Most of us have come to accept the fact that there is a structural deficit at the heart of our art form. It makes it self manifest mostly I would argue, in gender and/or racial terms. The biggest loser however is our culture as a whole. A culture that in the near fifty years I have been alive has moved to accept multi culturalism not as a bogie man or pipe dream but something that just simply is. But the organism we call modern Britain on the whole still trains its performing artist as if one homogenous lump. As if expression has to come through the lens of the dominant culture alone. To state the obvious does not. It cannot. Why? At the core of our ever-evolving culture are actors born to multiple identities. Able to serve multiple narratives with out ultimately privileging one of them.

In compiling this book Simelia has achieved some thing I perceive to be much needed. She is giving the said actor, to be specific the actor of colour as they say in the United States, access to express and investigate themselves through their multiple ever shifting identities. Which ultimately in my humble opinion fosters a greater sense of their national identity in the process. There has been much noise but the role of Black actor in contributing to a nations well being is a conversation that is only just really catching fire, but it is a fire that must burn.

I happen to believe that the actor reflecting truth might be the quickest way to introduce an idea into the consciousness of an audience. In order to access that truth, the actors must access every part of themselves. But they need sharpened contemporary tools to do that, or they grow up to be assembly line artists. Coloured versions of the same voice. These monologues are here to rebuke that. They are here to provoke the idea that all of the experiences of all of our peoples contribute equally to the articulation of our art. And that, I can only applaud. Read and enjoy.

Kwame Kwei-Armah
Playwright, and Artistic Director of the Centerstage Theatre in Baltimore, Maryland, USA

Performing Rights

Bombay Black by Anosh Irani
Playwrights Canada Press, 269 Richmond Street West, Suite 202, Toronto, Ontario, M5V 1X1, Canada, info@playwrightscanada. com
Excerpted from *Bombay Black* by Anosh Irani. Copyright © Anosh Irani 2006. Reprinted by permission of Playwrights Canada Press

A Brimful of Asha by Ravi Jain and Asha Jain
Playwrights Canada Press, 269 Richmond Street West, Suite 202, Toronto, Ontario, M5V 1X1, Canada, info@playwrightscanada. com
Excerpted from *A Brimful of Asha* by Asha Jain and Ravi Jain. Copyright © Asha Jain and Ravi Jain 2012. Reprinted by permission of Playwrights Canada Press

Child of the Divide by Sudha Bhuchar
By professionals to Tamasha, Rich Mix, 35–47 Bethnal Green Road, London E1 6LA, admin@tamasha.org.uk, and by amateurs to Permissions Department, Methuen Drama, Bloomsbury Publishing Plc, 50 Bedford Square, London WC1B 3DP, performance.permissions@bloomsbury.com
Copyright © Sudha Bhuchar 2006

Desert Sunrise by Misha Shulman
Misha Shulman, 610 East 7th Street, 1B, Brooklyn, NY, 11218, USA
Excerpted from *Salaam, Peace: An Anthology of Middle Eastern-American Drama*. Copyright © Misha Shulman 2009. Reprinted by permission of Theatre Communications Group

Detroit '67 by Dominique Morisseau
Paradigm Agency, 360 Park Avenue South, 16th Floor, New York, NY 10010, USA
Copyright © Dominique Morisseau 2013. Reprinted by kind permission of Oberon Books Ltd

The Elaborate Entrance of Chad Deity by Kristoffer Diaz
Samuel French, Inc., 45 West 25th Street, New York, NY 10010, USA
Excerpted from *The Elaborate Entrance of Chad Deity*. Copyright

The Empire by DC Moore

The Fever Chart by Naomi Wallace

Fireworks by Dalia Taha

Free Fall by Vinay Patel

Gone Too Far! By Bola Agbaje

Good Goods by Christina Anderson
Bret Adams Ltd., 448 W 44th Street, New York, NY 10036, www.
bretadamsltd.net
Copyright © Christina Anderson 2012

I Am Yusuf And This Is My Brother by Amir Nizar Zuabi
Judy Daish Associates Limited, 2 St Charles Place, London W10
6EG, licensing@judydaish.com
Copyright © Amir Nizar Zuabi 2010

I Call My Brothers by Jonas Hassen Khemiri
Rosica Colin Ltd., 1 Clareville St, South Kensington Underground
Station, London SW7 5AN
Copyright Jonas Hassen Khemiri © 2015; translation copyright ©
Rachel Willson-Broyles. Reprinted by kind permission of Oberon
Books Ltd

The Keepers of Infinite Space by Omar El-Khairy
Curtis Brown Group Ltd., Haymarket House, 28–29 Haymarket,
London SW1Y 4SP, info@curtisbrown.co.uk
Copyright © Omar El-Khairy 2014. Reprinted by kind permission
of Oberon Books Ltd

Moonfleece by Philip Ridley
Knight Hall Agency Ltd., Lower Ground Floor, 7 Mallow Street,
London EC1Y 8RQ, office@knighthallagency.com
Copyright © Philip Ridley 2010

The Mountaintop by Katori Hall
Creative Artists Agency, 162 Fifth Avenue, 6th Floor, New York,
NY 10010
Copyright © Katori Hall 2011

Mustafa by Naylah Ahmed
Nick Hern Books, The Glasshouse, 49a Goldhawk Road, London
W12 8QP, rights@nickhernbooks.co.uk
Copyright © Naylah Ahmed 2012. Reprinted by permission of Nick
Hern Books: www.nickhernbooks.co.uk

The North Pool by Rajiv Joseph
The Gersh Agency, 41 Madison Avenue, 33rd Floor, New York, NY 10010, info@gershla.com
Excerpted from *The North Pool*. Copyright © Rajiv Joseph 2013. Reprinted by permission of The Gersh Agency, 41 Madison Avenue, 33rd Floor, New York, NY 10010

Off the Endz by Bola Agbaje
United Agents LLP, 26 Lexington Street, London W1F 0LE, info@unitedagents.co.uk
Copyright © Bola Agbaje 2010

Red Velvet by Lolita Chakrabarti
Macnaughton Lord Representation, 44 South Molton Street, London W1K 5RT, info@mlrep.com
Copyright © Lolita Chakrabarti 2014

Refugee Boy by Benjamin Zephaniah adapted for stage by Lemn Sissay
Island Trading, 8 Kensington Park Road London W11 3BU
Original novel copyright © Benjamin Zephaniah 2001; adaptation copyright © Lemn Sissay 2013

rihannaboi95 by Jordan Tannahill
Marquis Entertainment, 312, 73 Richmond St W, Toronto, Ontario, Canada M5H 4E8, crivers@marquisent.ca
Copyright © Jordan Tannahill 2013. Reprinted by permission of Playwrights Canada Press

Snookered by Ishy Din
Julia Tyrrell Management Ltd., 57 Greenham Road, London N10 1LN, info@jtmanagement.co.uk
Copyright © Ishy Din 2012

Southbridge by Reginald Edmund
Robert A. Freedman Dramatic Agency, Inc., 1501 Broadway, Suite 2310, New York, NY 10036, info@robertfreedmanagency.com
Copyright © Reginald Edmund 2013. Reprinted by permission of the author

Sucker Punch by Roy Williams
Alan Brodie Representation, Paddock Suite, The Courtyard, 55
Charterhouse Street, London EC1M 6HA, abr@alanbrodie.com
Copyright © Roy Williams 2010, 2015

Ten Acrobats in an Amazing Leap of Faith by Yussef El Guindi
Gersh Agency, 41 Madison Ave, 33rd Floor, New York, NY 10010,
USA
Copyright © Yussef El Guindi 2005. Reprinted by permission of
the author

True Brits by Vinay Patel
Sayle Screen Ltd., 11 Jubilee Place, London SW3 3TD, info@
saylescreen.com
Copyright © Vinay Patel 2014

What Fatima Did … by Atiha Sen Gupta
Knight Hall Agency Ltd., Lower Ground Floor, 7 Mallow Street,
London, EC1Y 8RQ, office@knighthallagency.com
Copyright © Atiha Sen Gupta 2009. Reprinted by kind permission
of Oberon Books Ltd

**A Wolf in Snakeskin Shoes or The Gospel of Tartuffe by Marcus
Gardley**
William Morris Endeavor Entertainment, 1325 Avenue of the
Americas, 15th Floor, New York, NY10019, USA
Copyright © Marcus Gardley 2015

Every effort has been made to trace and acknowledge copyright
owners. If any right has been omitted the publishers offer their
apologies and will rectify this in subsequent editions following
notification.

Introduction

We owe it to ourselves to never stop learning about the wealth of talent which exists in our neighbourhoods, in our cities and around the world – so that we can understand ourselves, our ancestry and our community to empower, grow, celebrate and cultivate new ideas. This was my self-written mantra which became the springboard to create this anthology of monologues for Black, South Asian and Middle Eastern actors.

After troubleshooting and managing the Black Play Archive at the National Theatre – a digital resource initiated by Kwame Kwei-Armah, which consisted of professionally produced plays written by black British playwrights over the last seventy years – in addition to writing the first monologue anthology for black actors from black British plays, I had a strong desire to continue expanding my knowledge of plays for culturally diverse actors from British and international contemporary writers.

With support from Arts Council England, I travelled to the USA and London to carry out research in order to gather the material for this anthology. At every stop-off point, there was an immediate yet effortless ripple effect of communication, as the word about the forthcoming publication spread across the artistic communities internationally in person and over the internet, which enabled me to connect with practitioners, literary managers and producers based throughout London, Canada, New York, Chicago, Baltimore, Australia and Africa. I spent several months perusing personal and professional libraries, receiving recommendations from Kwame Kwei-Armah, Catherine Rodriguez, Gavin Witt, Betty Shamieh, Naomi Wallace, Ismail Khalidi, John Jack Patterson, Dalbir Singh and Raphael Martin, to name but a few. From practitioners, sales assistants at bookshops to audiences, everyone had a list of new, exciting and powerful contemporary plays which they urged me to read and select for this publication. Many are featured in this anthology, and the ones that never made the final draft have formed a place in my ever-growing play library, regularly feeding into the multiple programming conversations with directors and other theatre professionals.

Ironically, as I carried out the research for this collection from a place of celebration and love for my community, the same community was in uprising over the numerous accounts of the loss of innocent lives. This anthology was created against the backdrop of protests for social justice for Trayvon Martin, Michael Brown, Sandra Bland, the scarcely reported missing schoolgirls in Nigeria, the Charleston church shooting and the many innocent adults and children killed during the Israel–Gaza conflict – possibly the most painful time I have ever experienced in my entire life.

But as I read the works written by the ground-breaking contemporary writers featured in this anthology, it made sense of the chaos around me. Suddenly these local and worldly events were more real and personal. The people who were reported in the media were three-dimensional with feelings, backstories and families. The world that they lived in was depicted through our five senses and imagination, instantly transporting us to somewhere tangible and coherent. There is something quite special about exploring the world through the voices of contemporary writers who have the power to portray the world as they see it, and thus influence, educate, challenge, changing the hearts and minds of their audience, bringing healing and comfort to the community.

Bansky says 'Art should comfort the disturbed and disturb the comfortable', and through writing this anthology bursting with the work of contemporary writers who speak boldly and unapologetically about the world around them, it became clear to me the power, significance and reason for us to discover and champion those who tackle a diversity of themes, experiences and complex issues.

This anthology is a celebration of a diverse range of captivating and truly memorable leading male characters that represent the complexities of youth, masculinity, sexuality and race. The plays draw on our culturally rich theatrical tradition of storytelling, magical surrealism and spirituality, bringing both contemporary and historical stories to the foreground. These stories represent what it means to be a twenty-first-century man of colour, in business, at war and in life. With monologues from Roy Williams, Omar El-Khairy, Reginald Edmund, Jordan Tanahill, Kristoffer Diaz, Jonas Hassen Khemiri, DC Moore, Amir Nizar Zuabi and Marcus Youssef, the characters and themes are wide-ranging, with character journeys that cross cultural, political and historical boundaries.

The material has been arranged into age-specific groups: teens, twenties, thirties and forties-plus. Admittedly the playing age for some of the pieces was not specified by the author of the play. Therefore, I would strongly encourage you to break convention and take a playful approach by reading monologues outside of your age category; you never know what you may discover.

For the purpose of this book, I have included plays which have been published to encourage readers to invest in the full-length version of the plays (please refer to the publication list on page 155). I hope these monologues will inspire you to read further and discover more about the playwrights and plays they come from.

Discovering the plays featured in this anthology has been a wonderful learning experience for me; I hope actors from all over the world will embrace and enjoy this exploration of voices, experiences and themes.

Teens

From

SUCKER PUNCH

by Roy Williams

Sucker Punch received its world premiere at the Royal Court Jerwood Theatre Downstairs, Sloane Square, London on 11 June 2010. This production was directed by Sacha Wares, with the following cast: Daniel Kaluuya (Leon), Anthony Welsh (Troy), Jason Maza (Tommy), Nigel Lindsay (Charlie), Trevor Laird (Squid), Gary Beadle (Ray) and Sarah Ridgeway (Becky).

This critically acclaimed play was joint Alfred Fagon Award winner for Best New Play of the Year (2010), which included a staged reading at the National Theatre, Cottesloe Stage directed by Simeilia Hodge-Dallaway. The play was also nominated for the *Evening Standard* Award and the Olivier Award for Best New Play. Daniel Kaluuya, who played the protagonist, Leon, won both the 2010 Critics Circle and *Evening Standard* awards for Outstanding Newcomer.

Frank Bruno, Maurice Hope, Sugar Ray Leonard and Nigel Benn have one thing in common: they were all celebrated boxing champions from the eighties. Inspired by the many great boxing heroes of this decade, award-winning writer Roy Williams's play *Sucker Punch* shines a light on the relentless racism that these fighters had to endure before they battled with their opponents inside the ring. Racial tension was paramount in the early 1980s as a result of societal racism, poverty and oppressive policing which disproportionately targeted young black men under the 'sus law' (where anybody could be stopped and searched if officers merely suspected they might be planning to carry out a crime), which eventually led to a series of riots in black populated areas.

Sucker Punch is set in the 1980s. The play focuses on two young black British male protagonists: Leon Davidson and Troy Augustus. The pair get caught breaking into Charlie's (also known as Mr Maggs) run-down boxing gym and have to repay him by mopping the floor and cleaning the toilets. At the gym they are forced to contend with being called 'boy' by white trainer Charlie and racial slurs from Tommy (a racist boxer who is trained by Charlie). A fight erupts at the gym between Leon and Tommy, which is watched in the distance by Charlie, who sees that Leon has promise. Charlie decides to train Leon and Troy.

Leon falls for Charlie's daughter, Becky, and the two begin a relationship without Charlie's knowledge. When Charlie finds out, he is outraged at the idea of his daughter being in a relationship with a black man, and forces Leon to choose between the club and his daughter in an effort to break them up. Leon chooses the club.

An altercation with the police which results in Leon hiding out in Charlie's gym fractures the relationship between the two boxers. Troy confronts Leon for running out on him while he was getting harassed by the police for no reason. When Charlie attempts to intervene, Troy pushes him away and Charlie grabs his arm. Troy loses it. He is sick of being restrained by a white man. Charlie persists in calling Troy a 'boy', at which point Troy tells Charlie he is leaving the club. Troy looks to Leon for support, but Leon again chooses to stay with white trainer Charlie at the club.

Troy leaves for America in the belief that the black community is treated better over there, while Leon remains in London trying to assimilate into the white working-class community. They both accomplish boxing championship status.

Troy returns to London with a fake American accent and a controlling manager, to fight the biggest fight of all – against his former friend, Leon Davidson.

Summary (extract)

Sixteen-year-old **Leon** is set for his first amateur fight. His first taste of escapism. In desperate need of appreciation, love and acceptance from his white trainer **Charlie**, **Leon** enters the ring with a lot to prove. The crowd is cheering him on. But can **Leon** deliver?

Leon   The first fight I'm having is with some tall, skinny-looking kid. From the minute I step into the ring, he's staring me out, like I burgled his house. What am I doing here …? Oh! He lands one right on me. I'm going dizzy, I'm all numb. I wanna go home. I'll keep out of his way.

Bell rings.

Crowd seem to like it when I move around. I'll go a bit faster then. They're lapping it up. Let's see if they like this. Bop my shoulders, spin my arm like Sugar Ray Leonard, now they're cheering, can't get enough. Skinny white boy don't know what to do with me! I get in a jab, and it hurts him, my first punch as well. A bit of fancy footwork now, I think. Crowd are loving it. Another jab! Then a sweet uppercut! Skinny kid is down like a heap! I'm taking him out, me! My first ever fight, and I took him out. Fucking hell! Yes! What a feeling. Starting to like this. Next up is a fighter from Repton. Mark Saunders. Half-caste fighter from Brick Lane. Trying to find a way in here, but he's not having any of it. It's like he can see me coming. I go with the footwork. He can't keep up with me. I'm tiring him out, he's dazzled by my speed. That's it, that's it, keep him coming, keep him coming, now, have that!

He hits out with a flurry of punches.

Oh yes! I look to Charlie, he's gotta love it!

He takes a hit.

Oh that was stupid. All I can see is gloves, fuck, get me out! My ears are ringing. I've got pins and needles all inside, gotta take it, gotta keep up, make it to the next round, come on!

Ref stops the fight. Bell rings.

What? What … what the … what you mean he's won Ref? I didn't go down! I didn't go down, I was getting back up, I had him.

From

REFUGEE BOY

by Benjamin Zephaniah

Adapted for the stage by Lemn Sissay

A West Yorkshire Playhouse production, *Refugee Boy* was first performed at the West Yorkshire Playhouse, England on 9 March 2013, directed by Gail McIntyre and starring Fisayo Akinade (Alem Kelo), Rachel Caffrey (Ruth Fitzgerald), Andrew French (Mr Kelo), Dominic Gately (Mr Fitzgerald/Soldier/Assassin), Becky Hindley (Mrs Fitzgerald/Lawyer) and Dwayne Scantlebury (Mustapha/Sweeney/Judge). This production was subsequently followed by a national tour in February 2014.

Benjamin Zephaniah's acclaimed teen novel *Refugee Boy* was the recipient of the 2002 Portsmouth Book Award in the Longer Novel category. Based on a true story about two Ethiopian brothers who were left in a hotel room, Zephaniah's novel successfully gave voice to the unheard young refugee community. Lemn Sissay's adaptation of the novel, under the same title, brilliantly lifted the story from the page to the stage. We are taken on an emotional journey of a fourteen-year-old, mixed race Ethiopian-Eritrean teenage boy called Alem Kelo as he tries to adjust to life without his family in the UK, experiencing foster homes, seeking asylum and encountering discrimination. *Refugee Boy* is a heart-breaking story about the complexities of life as a refugee child – love, loss, hope and belonging.

Alem Kelo came to London with his father. Only, when he wakes up in a bed and breakfast hotel in Berkshire, he finds himself alone in an unfamiliar country. A note from his father is left for Alem, explaining his parents' hopes of protecting their child from a vicious civil war between Ethiopia and Eritrea, where they are rejected by both countries and receive daily threats to their lives due their mixed relationship. With no place of refuge, his Eritrean mother and Ethiopian father make the painful decision to leave Alem in London, while they work in Africa for peace between their homelands. Through the letters from his father, who promises to return to London to reunite with his son, and memories of his childhood with his family in Africa, Alem is able to remain strong and overcome adversity.

In London, with his family and homeland never far from his mind, Alem faces the new challenge of life as a refugee. From courtrooms to children's homes, he is at the mercy of social services and the legal system. At the children's home, Alem tries to fit in. Mustapha, who has a love for cars, takes Alem under his wing. But it is not long before he meets the bully of the home, Sweeney, and is subjected to his verbal and physical torment.

Things take a positive turn when Alem is placed in a loving foster home with the Fitzgeralds and their daughter Ruth. Alem receives another letter from his father, who informs him of his mother's death and his decision to return to London to be with his son. His dad arrives in London and seeks asylum and refugee status for both of them. They are rejected by the courts. With one chance to appeal, and with the support of his friends Mustapha, Ruth and Sweeney, Alem determines to take control of his life and to be seen as more than a Refugee Boy.

Summary (extract)

Fourteen-year-old **Alem** has been living with his foster parents for over two months – longer than the Fitzgeralds originally intended to foster him for. The courts have allowed **Alem** to stay with them until the next court hearing. **Mr Fitzgerald** is keen for **Alem** to move on after the hearing, but **Mrs Fitzgerald** is not so sure she's ready to let go.

A letter has arrived for **Alem** from his father and **Mr** and **Mrs Fitzgerald** deliberate whether to open it themselves or hand it over to **Alem**. They decided to give him the letter. **Alem** tentatively reads it aloud.

Alem   *reads the start of the letter to himself.* My dearest son,
I am afraid I have to tell you some very bad news. Remember
I told you in my last letter that darkness is upon the land? The
organisation of east has fallen apart and now there is not a single
organisation working for peace in the region. It seems that our
people are so busy dealing with war that there is no time to deal in
peace.

Well, my son, please prepare yourself for what I have to say. This
is very bad news because darkness is now upon our family. After
searching for many weeks I have just learned that your mother is
no longer with us. She was killed by some very evil people and
left near the border.

Please son, I want you to be strong, now I need you to be strong
more than ever, and your mother would want you to be strong. It
is very difficult for me here now, I don't feel that I have anything
here any more. It is dangerous here, too. Spies everywhere. So
soon enough I will be leaving here and joining you. At this time
I think that it is very important that we must be together so I am
coming. I will find you through the refugee council and we will be
together again.

I long to see you and I promise you I will be with you soon, so be
strong, be as strong as your mother and we will make it through
the darkness.

Bang! Bang! Bang! Bang! Bang! Bang!

There's someone at the door.

BANG! BANG! BANG!

Can't you hear them?

[**Mr Fitzerald** There's no one there, Alem.]

There is. There is.

[…]

Get off me. Get off me!!! Get off me!

BANG! BANG! BANG!

My father is coming. Don't you understand? My father is coming for me. He's here … He's here … Get the door.

BANG! BANG! BANG!

There's someone at the door.

From

GONE TOO FAR!

by Bola Agbaje

Gone Too Far! received its world premiere at Royal Court
Jerwood Theatre Upstairs in London on 2 February 2007. This
production was directed by Bijan Shebani with the following
cast: Marcus Onilude (Blazer), Tobi Bakare (Yemi), Tunji
Lucas (Ikudayisi), Bunmi Mojekwu (Paris/Mum), Zawe Ashton
(Armani), Ricci McLeod (Flamer), Ashley Chin (Razer), Maria
Charles (Old Lady), Munir Khardin (Shop Keeper/Policeman 1)
and Phillip Edgerley (Policeman 2).

British playwright, Bola Agbaje was inspired to write her debut
play *Gone Too Far!* after watching *The Gods Are Not to Blame* by
Ola Rotimi. Agbaje received critical acclaim for *Gone Too Far!*,
winning a 2008 Olivier Award for Outstanding Achievement.
The play draws on Agbaje's Nigerian-British identity, presenting
the complexities of cross-cultural upbringing in relation to racial
identity, cultural heritage and colonialism. It investigates why
a British-born teenager with Nigerian parents would readily
renounce his Nigerian heritage to adopt a more cool West Indian
identity, whilst living in a predominately black inner-city area.
Through this exploration, Agbaje boldly tackles the conflicts
within the black community, relating to complexion, cultural
disconnection and racial tensions between black African and West
Indian communities. *Gone Too Far!* deals with many heavyweight
themes which are cleverly addressed in a perfectly balanced
comedy drama.

Set on a council estate in South London, sixteen-year-old
London-born Yemi is looking forward to being reunited with his
estranged Nigerian older brother Ikudayisi (who was born and
raised in Nigeria). But when Yemi, a streetwise, fashion-conscious
young man, is confronted with a Yoruba-American-speaking
brother whose attire is a few months behind the current times, he
cannot hide his disappointment. Ashamed of his Nigerian heritage,
Yemi refuses to bond with his older brother.

When their mother sends them out on an errand to buy milk, Yemi fears his true Nigerian identity will be exposed to his friends and ruin his chances with his long-term crush, loud-mouthed Armani. Confronted with mixed-race Armani who discovers his Nigerian identity, Yemi's fears are realized when she unleashes an abundance of racially charged insults and derogatory name-calling. Yemi loses it and pokes Armani in the head. Armani is humiliated in front of her friend Paris and retaliates by running to her boyfriend Razer to initiate a fight between him and Yemi. Soft-spoken British West Indian Paris intervenes, trying to defuse the situation, which sparks a fight between the girls, with Armani accusing Paris of siding with the Africans and being jealous of her light-skinned complexion.

Ikudayisi tries to convince Yemi to be proud of his culture and native language, but Yemi is taught the true importance of embracing identity from the most unlikely resident of the estate, top gang member Blazer, a Yoruba-speaking Nigerian, just like his brother.

Summary (extract)

Estranged brothers **Yemi** (London-born) and **Ikudayisi** (Nigerian-born) are sent to buy milk for their mother. **Yemi** rejects his Nigerian heritage as well as his Nigerian brother. But when they bump into **Blazer**, a top South London gang member, who greets **Ikudayisi** in Yoruba, **Yemi** discovers that **Blazer** is no different from them. Eighteen-year-old **Blazer**, a well-dressed, intelligent young man who is both feared and respected on the estate, forces **Yemi** to accept his African identity and respect his older brother.

Blazer   Fuck what people think. You think I care? What da fuck can they try say to me? I'll have up any mans if they try to disrespect my tradition.

Pause.

You see me, yeah. I ain't ashamed of nothing.

Pause.

When I was younger, people used to take the piss out of me cos I had an accent. And it used to get me *mad*, but I never used to say nothing. But then one day I had enough and every man who tried to take the piss – got knocked out. Straight!

[…]

So what, you think now people will try take the piss with me now?

[…]

Exactly. It's not going to happen. They can say what they want behind my back, but to my face, mans have to be careful what they say. And that's the way I like it. Gone are da days when mans take the piss out of this African! Cos I run this estate now. And you know, I know they don't like it. But what can they do? The roles have reversed now.

[…]

I'm not saying to you, go around testing people. You just need to learn how to stand your ground, but keep it real at the same time. It's not a bad thing to be African. Be proud to be different.

[…]

Make sure you start to learn Yoruba from brother.

[…]

(*to* **Ikudayisi**)   Make sure you teach him.

[…]

(*to* **Yemi**)   Even if you want, blud, come round to mines, I will teach you. It's easy once you get started. (*To* **Ikudayisi**) And make sure you don't put on that fake accent again.

[…]

Oi.

[…]

(*to* **Yemi**)   What's your full name?

[…]

Do you know what it means?

[…]

Don't tell him. Let him find out himself – it would be a good lesson for him. That's your first assignment.

From

CHILD OF THE DIVIDE

by Sudha Bhuchar

Child of the Divide was co-produced by Tamasha Theatre
Company and Polka Theatre Company and received its world
premiere at Polka Theatre, London on 5 May 2006. This
production was directed by the former Artistic Director of
Tamasha Theatre Company, Kristine Landon-Smith, with the
following cast: Tony Jayawardena (Buttameez/Manohar Lal),
Rina Fatania (Hasina/Zainab), Divian Ladwa (Pali/Altaaf), Krupa
Pattani (Aisha/Kaushalya) and Amit Sharma (Pagal Head/Shakur).

Adapted from the short story *Pali* by Bhisham Sahni, *Child
of the Divide* by Sudha Bhuchar is a gripping and tragic story
about love, loss and belonging. The action takes place during the
most traumatic time in Indian history: the partition of India and
newly formed Pakistan, an event which led to a brutal massacre.
Told through the perspective of a Hindu child named Pali who
is separated from his father at the broader crossing during the
partition, Bhuchar's play conveys the physical, psychological and
emotional trauma, as well as the fears of the Hindu community.

A slip of the hand separates Pali from his father, leaving Pali
without a family or a home in a country where his life is in
danger. Muslim couple Zainab and Shakur, unable to conceive,
yearn to have a child of their own. When they find Pali, they
believe that faith has brought him into their lives and adopt him,
changing his name and faith to mask his Hindu identity. But what
starts out as an act of kindness quickly transpires into something
more profound.

Pali (now Altaaf) is allowed to play with the refugee children at
the camp, with new friends Hasina, who is also a love interest,
and Aisha. It is not long before they are confronted by local bully
Pagal Head and his sidekick, who is also Hasina and Aisha's
friend Buttameez. While the group are playing near Pali's former
family home, he speaks about his home and the truth about his
real identity is discovered by Pagal Head, who threatens to inform

his dad, a dangerous man who goes around killing Hindus. This revelation triggers Hasina to open up about her Pakistani-Hindu dual identity and the abuse she experienced from both sides. Pali realizes that he is not the only one living a lie.

Seven years later, his father returns to reunite Pali with his birth mother, who has mourned his lost since the day they parted. Pali must decide whether to leave the world he has now fully adjusted to or return to a new land with his biological family.

Summary (extract)

Pali overhears his adoptive parents resign themselves to the idea of letting him return to his biological parents and he runs away to **Buttameez**'s hideout. **Buttameez** used to live on the same campus as **Hasina** but successfully escaped to avoid being adopted. He now lives alone in a barn, talking to horses about his troubled life. **Pali** admires **Buttameez** for a life with no guidance from adults, but enigmatic **Buttameez**, who has become hardened to a lonely life, only wishes to have his family close. For the first time in the play, **Buttameez** lets his guard down to reveal the truth about his past.

Buttameez   (*hesitant as he tells his story*) All right then …
First when the bullets started flying over our heads, it was pure
fireworks … We'd play dodge-ball but it was like real bullets
… People said the white goras had drawn a line on the map and
now the Muslims had to go to a new country … Pakistan. I didn't
wanna go, but there was no choice … Before we could leave,
the Hindu mob came … I recognised our neighbour and Guddu's
dad … Guddu was like my best friend, you know … We traded
bante and swam in the river … My dad was brave … he could,
like, actually mash someone if they even said something about
his family … He just stood there … I saw them cut off his head
and set fire to the house … I climbed on the roof and jumped
into a pile of sugarcane chaff. They didn't see me … My legs. I
didn't feel the pain. I just hid there, covered in sugarcane skins
and licking them 'cos I was thirsty … and watched my family
burn inside … They were screamin' and that … at night, I started
walking straight … could hardly walk … kept asking people …
'Where is Pakistan? Which way?' I crossed the border but I never
saw no line.

[…]

No I'm no one's family. […] This old woman wanted me. She
said her house was my house. I said I got no family, I don't need
a house. And a schoolteacher said I could be his son but I didn't
want to. I'm bad luck.

[…]

Don't want to love anyone else. If you love people you lose them.

From

rihannaboi95

by Jordan Tannahill

rihannaboi95 is a unique live-streaming production, first produced by Suburban Beast, performed in an inner suburban Toronto bedroom and live-streamed to audiences' computers around the world on 23–28 April 2013. The production was directed by Zack Russell, featuring Owais Lightwala. The play was later revived by Downstage Theatre, live-streamed on the internet on 23 April–2 May 2015, directed by Simon Mallett, starring Diego Stredel (Sunny). *rihannaboi95* received a Dora Award for Best New Play, Theatre for Young Audiences division.

Jordan Tannahill's one-man play seamlessly merges theatre and the social media world to create one of the most powerful contemporary plays for young people. Written as a confessional YouTube video, this web-theatre play taps into our new age dependency on social media to feed our voyeuristic inquisitiveness, hunger for technological escapism and desire to be famous. But all is not glossy in the world of YouTube and Facebook, and Tannahill's hard-hitting play exposes the ruthless side of social media, where there's no hiding place for a sixteen-year-old boy whose lip-syncing/sissy boy dancing videos go viral. This is a heartbreaking story of how social media uploads left a teenage boy fearing for his life.

One click takes us into the life of a teenage boy named Sunny. The setting: a girl's bedroom, where Sunny is hiding out. As the story chronologically unfolds, we discover the events which have led a young Asian boy to flee his family home and take refuge in his friend's bedroom.

Sunny's face is bruised as he talks in a fast-paced energetic whisper to the lens of a video camera on the laptop. The story begins at high school where Sunny met his first crush, Mr Bailey. A class assignment on current news events inspires Sunny to focus on the turbulent relationship between his idol Rihanna and Chris Brown. Mr Bailey offers Sunny a laptop to enable him to complete his homework.

But at home, bored with writing a standard essay, Sunny has a better idea which he hopes will win the attention of Mr Bailey. With the assistance of his mother's umbrella, he decides to impress his teacher by recording a lip-synching video to Rihanna's song 'Umbrella'. Sunny accidently plays it, and watches it repeatedly, enjoying his great dance moves, just like Rihanna. The bell rings to indicate the end of class and as the students leave the classroom, Sunny prepares to reveal his video to Mr Bailey. His efforts are appreciated by his teacher, who encourages Sunny to continue making videos, which he does, in the unsafe environment of his conservative family home.

Sunny's videos become more experimental; he has now taken to applying make-up for the specially recorded performances from Rihanna's repertoire. As Sunny's obsession with creating lip-synching video increases, so does his infatuation with his teacher. He discovers that Mr Bailey is gay – the first gay man he has ever met. He begins to imagine the type of house Mr Bailey lives in and finds out Mr Bailey's home address, paying a visit without his teacher's knowledge.

Sunny wants more. Dissatisfied that only Mr Bailey is viewing his beautifully crafted videos, he posts them on YouTube. The feedback is overwhelming. The public responds positively and he begins to feel accepted and adored.

But things take a sudden turn for the worse when his videos are discovered by some of his classmates, his older brother and his parents. Sunny is left with no option but to run away, – but who can he turn to?

Summary (extract)

Sixteen-year-old high school student **Sunny** (whose online name is Rihannaboi) is a bit of a loner. His world changes when his lip-synching/sissy boy dancing home videos to Rihanna songs go viral, resulting in an abundance of hits, likes and a loyal cyber fan base. But when his classmates discover the videos, **Sunny** becomes the target for cyberbullying and physical and emotional abuse.

Sunny   Today started normal – breakfast, bus ride – until I get
to my locker and these boys, like, five grade-twelve boys come
up to me and start dancing right in my face, acting all gay and
doing Rihanna's moves in my face like right from my videos,
and they're singing 'I'm the only fag in the world', and I feel
everything begin to spin. They know. They've seen the videos.
How many? – maybe all of them. Good. Fuck them. Watch them
all for all I care. I grab my binder and start walking to class when
suddenly something hits the back of my head, almost knocks me
over. It's a pencil case. I pick it up and throw it back at them,
and so, yeah, I've never been a good thrower, and it falls like
way short and they just start laughing louder. In class it feels like
everyone's looking at me, whispering. Do they all know? How?
Whatever, I don't give a shit, three hundred of you gave me the
thumbs up, you think I care what they think? I pull up my hood
and slouch lower in my seat.

When the bell rings I run to my locker and there's a condom
taped to it. And there's spit in it. Or cum. Maybe real cum. But I
just peel it off and throw it on the ground like I don't even see it
'cause I can tell everyone in the hall's watching me, wanting me
to react, but I keep cool and undo my lock and take out my laptop
and nobody sees I'm crying: I don't want nobody to see so I run
into the washroom and I shut myself in the farthest stall and try to
connect to the Wi-Fi, even though the washrooms are like fucking
cement bunkers and have no reception, but YES finally I do – and
Facebook loads so slow but I can already see it: they found the
videos and posted them on my wall. And on their walls. And on
everyone's wall. Those boys from grade twelve – I think some of
them are friends with King. And they've even made a fan page for
me, with all my videos on it, guys and their girlfriends and their
friends posting sarcastic shit like, 'wow he's such an amazing
dancer', and 'Oh wow I would love to have sex with him he's so
sexy hummmmmm fuck my butt faggot'. And I punch the wall
with my fist and I scream 'cause it's concrete and I kick the door
again and again until it starts to break off the hinge. Good, let it
break. I want it to break.

From

WHAT FATIMA DID ...

by Atiha Sen Gupta

What Fatima Did ... premiered at the Hampstead Theatre in London on 22 October 2009. This production was directed by Kelly Wilkinson, with the following cast: Arsher Ali (Mohammed Merchant), Simon Coombs (Craig Johnson), Gethin Anthony (George Lewis), Bunmi Mojekwu (Stacey Clarke), Farzana Dua Elahe (Aisha Akbari), Catherine Cusack (Ms Harris) and Shobu Kapoor (Rukshana Merchant).

What Fatima Did ... is a funny and heart-wrenching story about the alienation faced by Muslim women who choose to wear the hijab. Gupta shines a light on the social attitudes of a multicultural Britain to expose feelings of contempt, misconceptions and lack of acceptance towards women who cover up. As the title implies, the play centres around the character Fatima, who is rarely seen on stage; we hear about her through the words of the people closest to her, a deliberate and clever choice of the author. We are therefore forced to painfully listen to the negative views of her so-called friends and family members. As her friends, boyfriend and mother turn against her, we begin to imagine how a young teenage girl is coping as her world begins to shrink. The only hope in the play comes from Fatima's twin brother Mohammed, who ultimately becomes the voice of reason and a compassionate source of strength for his sister.

Gupta's play allows us to see Muslim women who exercise their freedom of expression by choosing to wear the hijab as strong-minded, courageous and resilient.

The play begins on the first day back at school after a six-week summer holiday. The students of Green Park Comprehensive secondary school have not seen each since the last day of term. Fatima is late, as usual, and the other students jokingly place bets on the time she will arrive. As the teacher marks the register, a single knock at the door reveals Fatima in a hijab.

Like the rest of the class, Fatima's Irish boyfriend George is
convinced that she is playing a joke on everyone, and will return
to her old self – a girl who drinks, smokes and parties – before
the end of the school day. But when Fatima joins the group for
their after-school drinks at the pub dressed in the same attire and
ordering non-alcoholic beverages, George loses it and demands
that she takes off the hijab.

Fatima leaves the pub early. In her absence, her twin brother
Mohammed is in the firing line – the group want answers.
Mohammed supports his sister's decision to wear the hijab but
has to deal with the backlash from their unsupportive classmates.
He is accused of forcing her to wear the hijab. When he returns
home the fight continues. Mohammed's mother Rukshana, a feisty
Indian Muslim left-winger from a generation of women who have
fought against wearing the hijab, reveals to Mohammed that she
has given Fatima an ultimatum: the hijab or a place in the family
home.

Summary (extract)

Mohammed refuses to turn his back on his twin sister **Fatima**,
who has decided to wear the hijab. It's **Mohammed** and **Fatima**'s
eighteenth birthday, as well as the day on which **Fatima** has
to choose between living in the family home or wearing the
hijab. **Mohammed** is ironing his sister's hijab in the living
room; **Rukshana** (their mother) surprises him with a birthday
present. **Rukshana** sees the hijab and demands that her son
stops ironing it immediately. Determined to stop the rift in
his family home between his mother and sister, **Mohammed**
attempts to get his mother to understand what her children go
through on a daily basis in order for her to support her daughter's
decision.

Mohammed   (*Snapping.*) You don't know what it's like! Times
have changed! It's not about Paki this or Paki that. I understand
that. But it's not that. They don't even hate Asians anymore,
they hate us … specifically us … and I feel sick. Some days I
can barely go out on to the street, on the tube, to school without
feeling like my throat's gonna seize up. They look at us … they
know who we are and they hate us … the amount of fucking times
I've got on the train and people have moved away from me …
and I know exactly what's going on up here. (**Mohammed** *taps
his head.*) They're thinking that at least if they're in the further
part of the carriage, then when my bomb goes off, they'll lose a
leg or an arm – but not their lives. I know they're not getting up
to get off the train 'cos I watch them … I fucking watch them.
And they watch me watching them. And they NEVER get off at
the next stop. Never. And you wanna know the worse thing? They
give me that pathetic fucking I'm-ever-so-polite English half-smile
like this (**Mohammed** *demonstrates this smile*) before they move
away from me. (*Pause. Breathing in heavily.*) When you see a
white person with a backpack on, everyone thinks backpacker …
But when you see an Asian with a backpack on, you're only left
with terrorist. And that's what I'm saying. Why can't we all be
backpackers? Give me an answer and I'll be happy. I just want
an answer. (*Beat.*) And even though I would have never imagined
Fatima in a million years putting on the hijab before she did, I
don't blame her and I understand. I understand how she did it
even though I don't know why. (*Crying.*) I don't know why.

From

DESERT SUNRISE

by Misha Shulman

Desert Sunrise received its world premiere at Theater for the New City in New York, USA in September 2005. Due to the play's success, it was revived the following year in April 2006. Both productions were directed by the playwright, Misha Shulman, with the following cast: Aubrey Levy (Tsahi), Haythem Noor (Ismail), Alice Borman (Layla), Yifat Sharabi (Soldier 1), Morteza Tavakoli (Soldier 2), Yoel Ben-Simhon (Chorus/Musician) and Bhavani Lee (Dancer). The play was later produced at Northwestern University in Chicago and the Lillian Theatre in Los Angeles.

New-York-based Jerusalem writer Misha Shulman draws on facts and real-life events in a fictitious story, *Desert Sunrise*. Set in the South Hebron Hills in a shallow wadi on the Israeli-occupied West Bank, the writer brings together unlikely characters – an Israeli soldier, a Palestinian shepherd and a troubled young Arab woman – to make a statement about the war, humanity and friendship. Throughout the play a chorus and a musician complement the action and accompany the actors' dances and songs. The play effortlessly combines comedy, music, poetry and dance to tell a tragic, but yet hopeful story.

The action takes place over one night and opens with the gun of Tsahi, an off-duty Israeli soldier, pointed at drum-playing Palestinian shepherd Ismail. In a world where nobody is to be trusted, a lost Tsahi is forced to ask the only person present to steer him in the right direction. The two men, both equally suspicious of each other's motives, enter into a strained conversation based on propaganda-incited generalizations. It becomes clear that their preconceptions of each other are unfounded and they weaken their guards to proceed into everyday light-hearted conversation and banter.

Tsahi opens up about his recent separation from his girlfriend and Ismail discloses his plans to propose to the love of his life, Layla, on her arrival. While they wait for Layla, Tsahi teaches Ismail how to slow dance like they do in the American movies, so that he can slow dance with Layla. Tsahi encourages Ismail to pretend that he is Layla as they dance, and a rigid Ismail begins to let go of his inhibitions, just as Layla enters. As she watches the two men dancing, a horrified and confused Layla picks up Tsahi's rifle and orders him to let Ismail go.

Layla, who is considered a rebel girl because of her pride, revives the fear and terror of the opening scene, not knowing what or who to trust. Layla reminds Ismail about the recent suffering inflicted on both their families by the Israelis which, unlike Ismail, she cannot forget or forgive as easily.

As we draw deeper into the night, Layla's mental state becomes even more alarming, her dialogue fluctuating between logic and incomprehensible riddles about death. The men hear gunshots and shouting in the near distance and prepare for confrontation. As Ismail fights to get Layla to follow his instructions, Tsahi accidently fires his gun, causing a retaliation of random gunshots with fatal consequences.

Summary (extract)

A young Israeli soldier **Tsahi** has a heated argument with rebellious strong-willed Palestinian **Layla**, who is adamant to go against her father's wishes and attend university. **Layla** accuses her father and **Tsahi** of being fearful of women. She threatens to fight **Tsahi** and the Israeli people, and ends her rant by spitting at **Tsahi**'s feet, which sends **Tsahi** into a fit of rage. He slaps **Layla** in her face and is thrown to the ground and kicked in the stomach by new friend **Ismail**. **Ismail** breaks the silence to asks **Tsahi** if he's okay. **Tsahi** turns around, his eyes red with tears. The altercation with **Layla** has triggered a past memory involving another determined woman – his sister.

Tsahi (*from the Hebrew name Yitzhak, Isaac*)   Your woman, she reminds me of my sister.

I saw her spit once. At my father's feet. That was the only time he ever slapped her. But it didn't help. She went and did just what he forbade her to do, and never came back.

[she was going] To a pub. In Ramallah. It was called Brivacy. With a B. It was like no pub in Jerusalem. A pub only for women. My father told her not to go. He didn't know where it was, he only knew what kind of pub it was, and that was enough. He told her that he raised her to be a woman, not a man. They yelled and screamed at each other. She was crying, my big sister. *Tsipi*. But through her tears I could see her black eyes blazing with fire, and she shot her words at him like bullets. "You love me only in your chains. You don't love *me*. You despise my nature." "I despise your choices", my father said. "That's right," she answered, "you like it when I have none to make." My mother tried to calm her down, but she just got more violent. "Don't talk to me, Mother, my freedom is your worst nightmare." I stood in the corner and through my little ten-year-old eyes I watched my family rip itself apart, and did nothing. A terrible fear came over me, as if death were outside our door, waiting. (*He walks towards* **Layla***. He speaks to her without anger.*) My father told her she is a disgrace to her family and a disgrace to women. That was when she spat at his feet, and stood there in front of him waiting to be slapped, like a lion cub waiting to be fed. (*Layla walks away from him.*) After he slapped her, he told her to leave. She walked out, leaving the door open. (*Again he walks towards* **Layla***.*) I ran to the door and called her name. She turned and looked at me, her dark green dress shining in the moonlight. "*Tsipi, Al telchi,*" I said. "Don't go." She walked towards me and, trying to smile through her tears, said, "It's time for me to go." (**Layla** *sits next to* **Ismail***.*) When she turned around and started walking I wanted to run after her. (*To* **Ismail***.*) But I was too afraid to leave the house.

(*Pause.*)

We didn't hear from her for months. Finally the police contacted my parents. Her body was found in a wadi halfway between Jerulsalem and Ramallah. She had been stabbed all over.

From

THE NORTH POOL

by Rajiv Joseph

The North Pool received its world premiere at Theatreworks
Silicon Valley in Palo Alto, California on 13 March 2011.
This production was directed by Giovanna Sardelli, with the
following cast: Adam Poss (Khadim Asmaan) and Remi Sandri
(Dr. Danielson). The play received its US East Coast premiere at
Barrington Stage Company in Pittsfield, Massachusetts on 29 July
2012, directed by Giovanna Sardelli and starring Babak Tafti
(Khadim Asmaan) and Remi Sandri (Dr. Danielson).

The North Pool is a gripping cat-and-mouse psychological thriller
by Pulitzer Prize finalist, Ravij Joseph. This two-hander explores
the anti-Islamic views in America after the start of the war in Iraq.
With growing mistrust, scrutiny and paranoia in the community,
the play examines how these feelings manifest themselves in
an everyday environment – an average American high school
(Sheffield Academy), where the new kid on the register is an
eighteen-year-old Middle Eastern boy named Khadim.

Khadim has no idea why he has been called to the Vice Principal's
office on the last day of term before spring break. But it's clear
that he has done something wrong. Dr. Danielson – a boastful man
whose life is ruled by facts, statistics, and a self-written mantra,
'Pride of work, pride of self' – casually questions Khadim about
his voting in the school election, his reason for leaving the cross-
country running team, his family and his whereabouts last Tuesday
during his French class with Madame Friedman, who marked
Khadim as unexcused absence on the register.

Khadim answers convincingly. But Dr. Danielson has been
keeping a close eye on the Middle Eastern student since he
joined the school and has evidence to prove Khadim is lying. The
punishment is an hour's detention with the Vice Principal, which
Khadim chooses to serve immediately. The detention plays out in
real time.

The plot thickens. The questions darken to an interrogation about the recent suicide of Lia Winston, a promising flute player who killed herself after a sex tape scandal. Khadim is the main suspect. But Khadim also has reason to believe that Dr. Danielson is not without sin; besides, he had access to the sex tape and was the last person to see Lia before she died.

The play suddenly takes an unlikely turn as dark secrets are revealed and a plea for forgiveness is on the lips of Dr. Danielson.

Summary (extract)

Eighteen-year-old **Khadim** is held in detention for an hour in the Vice Principal **Dr. Danielson**'s office for skipping **Madame Friedman**'s French class. After several minutes of relentless questioning from **Dr. Danielson** regarding his personal life and recent activities, a pink mobile phone is placed on the table. It belongs to **Lia Winston**, a friend of **Khadim**'s, who committed suicide after a sex tape scandal. The mobile phone was left by a battered **Lia** in **Dr. Danielson**'s office on the day she died. The last text on her phone was to **Khadim**, telling him to get out of her life. **Khadim** was the last person to call her. **Dr. Danielson** wants answers. **Khadim** is forced to tell the truth.

Khadim   She needed money. She didn't have any money.

She knew I could get her money.

I know people who …
Kids who …
(*Beat*.) These kids I know from Riyadh. Saudi kids, oil kids.
Way more money than me, and they throw these parties …
And they like to bring in girls to be there, you know, to just wear a
little dress and be sexy and get all fucked up with them.
I told Lia about it, but not to …
I didn't tell her about it so she would go there and do that!
I told her because it was crazy. And Lia, she loved hearing about
everything, all the stuff I've seen in my life, you know? She liked
hearing about the world.
But once she heard about these parties, she was intent.
She would get intent on something, you know?
She needed money.
And they were going to pay her five thousand dollars to go to
a *party*. She knew the deal. That sex tape was her resume, you
know? She made me give them the tape.
She knew what she was getting into.

(*Becoming more upset*.) I wasn't there, I told you …
I don't get invited to those parties.
She went to it. It went all night long.

I don't know. I don't know what happened.
She called me at like five in the morning. She was … She wanted
me to come pick her up, and I went out to get her. She told me
some corner that wasn't anywhere near the party. I don't know
how she got there, I don't know what happened to her. And I kept
having to call her back 'cause I couldn't find her. She'd say she
was some place and then she wouldn't be there. She'd say she was
some other place, she wouldn't be there. And I was just driving
around in circles.
And then finally she was there. On some corner, in her little dress
and no shoes and her feet were all dirty.
She just got in and didn't say anything the whole way home.
I couldn't even look at her.

I wanted to tell her …
I wanted to say to her …
(*Beat.*) I pulled up to her dad's house. Her dad's shit-ass fucking piece-of-shit house and she got out.

(*Beat.*)

She said she got double the money because of her face.

Khadim *looks at the flute on the desk.*

Then I bought her that stupid flute.
I told her I bought it and she was like, *how can I play the flute with my mouth like this?*
I told her it would heal.
I was supposed to meet her at our spot, in the park, by the cliff.
And I got there late. I was late. And she wasn't there, and I waited and waited and I started calling her.

He takes her cell phone from **Danielson** *and opens it. Stares at it.*

I called her and I called her and I …
I still do.
In the middle of the night or …
In the middle of the day. I call her. I call her. Her voice still answers.

A very long silence. Neither man knows what to do or say. The argument, the fight, seems to be a dream they are both walking from.

(*Quietly*) I have to go.

But **Khadim** *makes no move to leave.*

From

I AM YUSUF AND THIS IS MY BROTHER

by Amir Nizar Zuabi

I Am Yusuf And This Is My Brother was first performed at the Al
Midan Theatre, Haifa on 24 September 2009, followed by a tour
to towns and villages in Galilee and the West Bank. The following
year, Palestinian theatre company ShiberHur collaborated with
the Young Vic Theatre in London to produce *I Am Yusuf ...* at the
Young Vic Theatre on 19 January 2010, directed by Amir Nizar
Zubai with the following cast: Ali Suliman (Ali), Amer Hlehel
(Yusuf), Paul Fox (Rufus), Salwa Nakkara (Old Nada/Woman
from different time/Um Samar/ Water woman/Dead refugee),
Samaa Wakeem (Nada/Water woman/Dead refugee), Taher Najib
(Nagi/Water woman/Dead refugee), Tarez Sliman (Girl from
Haifa/Water woman/Dead refugee), Yussef Abu Warda (Old Yusuf/
Man with tree/Man from Haifa).

I Am Yusuf is a beautifully written tragedy which tells a story of
brotherhood, love and sacrifice. Performed in English and Arabic,
this politically charged play boldly places the unheard stories of
the Palestinian community at the forefront as we follow the lives
of two young Palestinian brothers, Ali and Yusuf. Amir Nizar
Zuabi deliberately sets the play in 1948 during the Palestinian
war (al-Nakba), which resulted in over 700,000 Palestinians being
banished from their homeland, to commemorate the experiences of
the displaced Palestinian community, capturing their fears, losses
and memories. Through the perspective of the younger Palestinian
community, we see how the end of the British Mandate, the UN
partition vote and the aftermath of the election impacted on the
brothers and the rest of their community.

The play takes place in the Galilee village of Baissamoon, in an
area called Ramallah. At the heart of the play is an ill-fated love
story between Ali and Nada, who desire to be married. However,
due to Ali's good-hearted but simple brother Yusuf, Nada's
father objects to their marriage for fear that their children will
turn out like Yusuf. This causes a love/hate relationship between

the brothers. Ali is both protector and bully – quick to lash out violently towards Yusuf, who never fights back. Ironically, the love that Ali has for Yusuf is undeniable. We come to realize that Yusuf's infantile behaviour is the fault of Ali, who convinced his brother to lean over a dry well, causing Yusuf to fall head-first and crack open his head. The guilt eats away at Ali, who feels responsible but yet burdened by their co-dependent relationship. As the play unfolds, we (the audience) see glimpses of Yusuf's brilliance; unbeknown to Ali, Yusuf is not as simple as he looks.

Ali tries tirelessly to convince Nada's father to change his mind, but his efforts are wasted on Nada's stubborn and dangerous father. After being insulted by Ali (who calls him a coward), he responds by dragging his daughter by her hair through the village. Nada and Ali plot to run away together, but are stopped prematurely when Nada receives news that her father has been killed. Ali becomes the main suspect, and Nada begins to doubt the man she loves.

As the love of Ali's life walks away, society is changing politically. The British Mandate is coming to an end. Rufus, a soldier with the occupying British forces, is anticipating the 'best day of his life': 15 May 1948, the date of the progressive withdrawal of the British armed forces. He has never been more ready to detach himself from the problems caused by the British, to continue a carefree life in Sheffield. The UN elections have revealed that America, along with 32 other countries, has favoured the partition plans to create two states, one Jewish and one Arab, in Palestine. In two weeks' time the civil war will break out, leaving Ali, Yusuf and Nada fearing for their lives and contemplating their next move. Nada is keen to leave, but Ali is determined to fight for his land.

Summary (extract)

The scene takes place on 25 June 1948. The attack on Baissamoon has begun. **Yusuf**, a good-hearted but simple man, is surrounded by shooting bullets, but he is unable to move. He stands alone, recounting his first experience of the civil war.

Yusuf *doesn't move. Bullets whistle by. He still doesn't move.* **Old Yusuf** *passes through slowly.*

The south army is fighting the north army and the wind blows.

Where is everyone? Hiding in the bushes?

The leaves on the trees are fighting gravity and the wind is fighting the branches

And the urge to howl

Now the army is attacking from all fronts!

The wheatsheaves fight against their ripeness and the hard working ants.

The stone walls of our houses fight the salt in our tears and the shrubs.

The rain is attacking tears

And the white of our bones bleaches the whiteness of the clouds …

Where is everyone? Running through the olive groves?

The tank is attacking the rice on our plates

And the bitter coffee in our tiny rattling cups.

The cows attack the grass and the grass gives shelter to the dead.

The sheep attack our wool coats and the shepherd on the cross

And the donkeys resist forgetfulness with stubbornness.

The machine gun is spreading sesame on my grandmother's bread

And her warm greeting to a passing guest.

Where is everyone? Hiding in the wells?

The airplanes are fighting the butterflies

And the silver mosquitoes swarm round the eyes of the dead dog.

The hungry children bite off their elbows to attack their empty stomachs.

The marching army attacks the snakes in the fields with the stomp of their boots

And the hand grenade attacks the hands and the orange fruits on the trees.

Mice attack the flour sacks.

Flowers attack the graves.

Where is everyone? Hiding under their beds?

The bullets race the wasps and my heart is racing its galloping horses

And the pigeons swirl round the white flags that were my mother's dowry sheets

And the blushing blood of her purity is washed by the black blood of dead hens.

Where is everyone? Gone to the dust and the tents over the hills?

Where is everyone? Where are the smells of cooking food?

Where are the greetings and good mornings of this dawn?

Where are the villagers with their sourdough dreams?

Where is everyone? Am I alone? Had time ended?

Is it the beginning? When will it end?

From

THE KEEPERS OF INFINITE SPACE

by Omar El-Khairy

The Keepers of Infinite Space was first performed at the Park
Theatre, London on 22 January 2014. It was produced by Moving
Theatre in association with Global Uncertainties, developed and
directed by Zoe Lafferty, with the following cast: Philip Correia
(Shadi), Edmund Kingsley (Saeed), Laura Prior (Yael/Sara/Claire),
Hilton McRae (Khalil), John Wark (Abner), Cornelius Macarthy
(Ziv/Tom), Sirine Saba (Haneen/Asma), Patrick Toomey (Takek/
Muhib).

Omar El-Khairy's harrowing drama about Palestinians in the
Israeli prison system is set after the Israeli occupation of 1967.
El-Khairy focuses on the continued political corruption, criminal
injustice and brutality inflicted on the prisoners, as well as the
impact on families and communities, in a play which spans over
three decades, 1990–2012. *The Keepers of Infinite Space* is a
political drama about family, betrayal and injustice.

As Khalil, a property developer, stands in a conference room
selling his vision for a new Palestine, his son Saeed, a twenty-
eight-year-old bookseller, is arrested and placed in an Israeli
military holding cell without a substantial reason. Saeed's screams
to be released fall upon the deaf ears of the Israeli prison guards,
who take pleasure in inflicting torture on him. Taken from the
cell to the interrogation room, a shackled Saeed is questioned
by narcissist Israeli defence force officer Abner, control-freak
Israeli guard Yael, and first-day-on-the-job Ethiopian prison guard
Ziv. Prison officer Ziv is trained by the infamous Abner, who
has a clear instruction to ensure the prisoners are treated not as
humans but as objects – a table. Ziv is encouraged to ridicule and
humiliate his new prisoner, showing no mercy or forgiveness.
Saeed's punishment for disobeying the guards is time in isolation
and an extended sentence.

Meanwhile, Khalil's conference is interrupted when he is informed
of his son's current situation, leaving Khalil shaken with despair.

The charge still unknown, Saeed is sentenced to forty days by the prison guards. Relentless trips back and forth from the holding cell to the interrogation room reveal the real reason for his incarceration. The interrogation starts to focus on his resistance fighter brother, as the guards want to track him down. A loyal Saeed refuses to disclose his brother's whereabouts.

Saeed's only visitor is his wife, who tries to keep his business alive against the odds. She becomes his hope and reason to survive. But away from the visitors' room, Saeed is subjected to spies, addictive drugs and solitary confinement, which slowly ebb away at his ability to think logically.

As months turn into years and still no visit from his father, Saeed's suspicion grows. In the prison cell he meets other prisoners, including the top dog, Muhib, who is able to get mobile phones, porn and cigarettes. Muhib reveals dark secrets about Saeed's father. Surrounded by prisoners who have been incarcerated for over fourteen years without trial, Saeed realizes that the only way to escape the Israeli prison is death or breaking out.

Summary (extract)

Sixteen-year-old **Shadi** is the youngest Palestinian prisoner in the cell, incarcerated for throwing rocks at Israeli soldiers during a demonstration. Due to his age, **Shadi** is visited and interviewed by **Tom**, a British International Committee of the Red Cross aid worker from Slough, England. With **Shadi**'s father working in an ice-cream shop in Ramallah, the two share a love of ice-cream. But that is all. They have different experiences of the Middle East. Tom has a Masters' Degree in Near and Middle Eastern Studies together with wide-eyed ambitions to help **Shadi** under the Fourth Geneva Convention, while **Shadi** has lived and fought against the conflict, having lost close relatives along the way. **Shadi** astutely identifies that **Tom**'s efforts are redundant, but reluctantly agrees to tell his story.

Shadi   (*Beat.*) He loved pistachio.

(*Beat.*) I hung in the air – blood dripping from my body. My shirt covered in blood. My whole body shaking. I remember feeling numb – from the shrapnel that hit me in the thigh.

We were at this demonstration. My brother, Abed – he was – was standing right next to me. I'd told him not to come, but he wouldn't listen.

He was hit straight in the head with a tear-gas canister.

'There was no change nor strength except through Allah, to Allah we belong, and to Him we will return.'

That's all I remember him saying – my father.

Pause.

It was sometime in the morning – three – four, maybe. I heard this loud bang – then the sudden stench of gas. There was a flood of soldiers into the house. My mother began shouting, and then I felt someone grab me and rip me out of bed. The soldiers took me outside – to their jeep. My mother followed them – lashing out and screaming. (*Beat.*) But my father – he just stood there – in the doorway. Silent.

That's the last time I saw them.

I was undressed and left standing in my underwear. They dragged me for interrogation. They beat me. They beat you hard in those first few days because they know no one's going to see you – or the bruises. And this carried on for days. I don't really know how long. Question after question. I was real hungry – starving. I told them, but they just said I could eat once I'd confessed.

They put me in this room. It kept going from hot to cold – freezing to boiling. I don't know how they did it. Then, after a few hours, I started to feel my heart beating faster and faster. I shouted for them to let me out. Nothing. I thought my heart was going to explode at any moment.

A few days later they showed me this video of children throwing stones at soldiers – and – (*Beat.*) And I admitted – that I was one of them. One of the kids in the video.

It wasn't me though – in the video. I just had to – you know.

(*Beat.*) And what are you going to do with that testimony, Tom? (*Beat.*) Give it to your superiors? (*Beat.*) And what do you think they're going to do with it? (*Beat.*) You're just wasting your time, my friend.

Twenties

From

RED VELVET

by Lolita Chakrabarti

Red Velvet received its world premiere at the Tricycle Theatre
in London on 11 October 2012, directed by the Tricycle's
artistic director Indhu Rubasingham with the following cast:
Adrian Lester (Ira Aldridge), Ferdinand Kingsley (Casimir/
Henry Forrester/Halina Wozniak/Betty Lovell), Rachel Finnegan
(Margaret Aldridge), Simon Chandler (Bernard Warde/Terence),
Natasha Gordon (Connie), Ryan Kiggell (Charles Kean), Charlotte
Lucas (Ellen Tree) and Eugene O'Hare (Pierre Laporte).

Lolita Chakrabarti won awards for her critically acclaimed play,
including Most Promising Playwright at the *Evening Standard*
Awards and the Critics' Circle Awards for the 2012 run of *Red
Velvet*. Actor Adrian Lester, who played Ira Aldridge, also won a
Critics' Circle Award for Best Actor.

Red Velvet resurrects one of the most pioneering and yet almost-
forgotten black actors in British theatre history. African-American
actor Ira Aldridge, noted as the first black actor to play Othello
and renowned for playing many Shakespearean roles in the
early nineteenth century, takes centre stage once more in Lolita
Chakrabarti's riveting play – an imagined story of Aldridge's life
based on true events. Set in a period when slavery still existed
in America and England was debating the abolition of slavery
in British colonies, Chakrabarti's play shows how a black actor
triumphs against racism to achieve his dreams of becoming
one of the greatest Shakespearean actors on the British stage.
Through unearthing the story of Ira Aldridge, Chakrabarti makes
a commentary on the politics of theatre and the ingrained racism
which still exists.

Red Velvet unravels the mystery of why Ira Aldridge never
returned to London after his revolutionary performance of Othello
in Covent Garden in 1833. The play begins in 1867, the same
year that Aldridge died. Aldridge is in a theatre dressing room in
Łódź, Poland, preparing to play King Lear. A young, enthusiastic

and insistent Polish journalist, Halina, interviews a dying Aldridge about his career, family and why, after over thirty years, he still has not returned to London.

The play goes back in time to 1833 as we witness the events leading to Aldridge's departure from London. As the sounds of the protest over the abolition of slavery are heard outside, the *Othello* cast gather on the stage of the Theatre Royal in Covent Garden. The revered leading actor, Edmund Kean, has collapsed on stage while performing the role of Othello, and the cast talk distressingly about the unfortunate situation, not knowing who will replace him. Theatre manager, Frenchman Pierre Laporte arrives at the theatre with a young black American actor, and to the cast's disdain announces that Ira Aldridge will become the new Othello, a role previously played by white actors usually in black face.

This bold and shocking revelation is defied by the cast (especially Edmund Kean's son, who plays Iago) and Aldridge's performance is slaughtered by the press, which leads to the temporary closure of the theatre.

Summary (extract)

An elated twenty-six-year-old **Ira** is on the stage of the theatre after his second appearance in the role of Othello. He has given the best performance of his life, but theatre manager and friend **Pierre** is not happy with **Ira**'s choice to play the part hard and fierce against his request for a more gentle approach. To make matters worse, **Edmund Kean**'s son has made allegations that his fiancée **Ellen**, who plays alongside **Ira**, has incurred bruises during the performance.

The case against **Ira** mounts as **Pierre** declares the board's decision for **Ira** to step down. **Ira** wants them to fight the board, but **Pierre** is unprepared to defy a team of men who control the theatre establishment and media. **Pierre** calls his decision to cast **Ira** a mistake, siding with the board.

A deflated and wounded **Ira** realizes that he is completely alone. For the first time in the play, **Ira** talks about the personal and political challenges he had to battle throughout his career.

Ira   I finally did it. Said I'd pay his passage. That he should
come … see that I'm here. Ten years, Pierre, ten years without one
word and here I am, finally, with something to say …

[…]

He tol' me that 'actin' was 'gainst nature, not true work for a man
o'god.' … You wanna know what he really does for a livin' when
he's not preachin'? He sells straw. In a horse and cart he has to
rent for the privilege, up and down, up and down callin' 'straw!'
Can you imagine …? And my mama, god rest her weary soul,
scrubbed floors. You got a floor, Pierre, my mama would've buff it
up fine.

[…]

'Salesman' seemed to cover it and well, you never asked. Look, you
and I, we don't have the ease of following in footsteps. We stand
apart, I see that. It's a, a lonely path and putting your head above the
parapet is a, it's a courageous thing […] When I was a boy, there
was this man, William Brown, he had no one to follow. Spent his
life savings on a house, rundown, basic but he had such passion he
turned that house into a theatre. He would serve cakes and punch in
the back yard in the interval. His friend, Jimmy Hewlett, was an actor
– untrained, unpolished, worked as a tailor uptown in the day but was
burnin' up with talent. They dared too, Pierre. You see Jimmy was
cuttin' an' stitchin' in the day. Mr Brown did odd jobs, I was at school
but evenings we rehearsed and played *Romeo and Juliet*, *Richard
III*, *Henry V*. I was fourteen. We were rough but we had passion …
and we became real popular. Powers that be didn't like it though
and one night while we playin' in our tumbledown theatre and our
homemade costumes, they set fire to that house. It burned like paper.
The drier the wood, the quicker it burns. The noise was deafenin' –
screams, the flames catchin' further, shoutin'. Couldn't see my way
out, couldn't breathe and just when I thought I was done, Mr Brown
grabbed my hand, pulled me up from the floor and dragged me out
into the open air and look what he did. We just in the fire, Pierre
… I've given everything to get here. I have pushed and forced and
played my way in.

[…]

Don't you find it edifyin', Pierre, that no one bats an eye when grandma plays Juliet and that we all applaud the East End drunk as the warrior Moor? So when Kean plays the Moor, we're amazed at how skilfully he descends into this base African tragedy but with me it seems I'm revealin' my true nature. And the most illuminatin' thing for me is that you're standin' on the other side. The radical red cap son of the revolution hand in hand with the blue blood brigade.

[...]

Damn you!

From

MOONFLEECE

by Philip Ridley

Moonfleece received its world premiere at Rich Mix in London
on 3 March 2010, directed by David Mercatali with the following
cast: Beru Tessema (Zak), Reece Noi (Link), Emily Plumtree
(Sarah), Ashley George (Gavin), Sian Robins-Grace (Nina),
Bradley Taylor (Tommy), Sean Verey (Curtis), Reeda Harris
(Wayne), Krupa Pattani (Alex), Alicia Davies (Stacey) and David
Ames (Jez).

Philip Ridley is a controversial playwright who is constantly
pushing boundaries; *Moonfleece* is a prime example of Ridley's
efforts to use his art to challenge the minds of our community. The
play boldly tackles the subjects of racism and homophobia. The
play toured to tour the production to areas with a high population
of British National Party followers, namely Bradford, Leicester,
Birmingham, Doncaster and Dudley. It was subsequently
banned from Dudley's Mill Theatre, due to the venue fearing the
community's disapproval. *Moonfleece* was specifically written
for young people to speak to the younger supporters of extreme
right-wing parties. Ridley brilliantly uses drama, fairy tale, fantasy
and comedy to create a powerful, hard-hitting play.

Moonfleece is set in East London and tells the story of Curtis, a
young, troubled, right-wing activist, who has arranged a meeting
with his party members and ex-girlfriend Sarah at a derelict flat
in an abandoned high-rise building. Curtis arrives to find the flat
occupied by squatters, Link and Zak. Angered by the squatters
who refuse to leave the premises, Curtis reveals his long-standing
connection with the flat, which was once his family home.

Things become even more upsetting for Curtis when his
ex-girlfriend Sarah appears with her outspoken South Asian friend
Alex, gay student journalist Jez, who takes an interest in Curtis,
and wheelchair-bound psychic Nina, who uses every opportunity
to flirt with Curtis's best friend and fascist party activist Tommy.

But something more prevalent is haunting Curtis. Since the death of his brother, he has been seeing his ghost, which is why he organized the meeting. The group gather enough chairs to cater for everyone to carry out a séance. But Zak has a hidden secret about Curtis's brother, which will change Curtis's views on his family forever.

Summary (extract)

Twenty-two-year-old **Zak** wears jeans, boots, T-shirt and a jacket decorated with silver studs and paint which belonged to **Curtis**'s deceased brother, **Jason**. **Curtis** wants to know how **Zak** got **Jason**'s jacket, but **Zak** is adamant to keep his promise to **Jason** by not telling **Curtis** the truth about the events leading to his brother's death.

After much pressure from **Curtis** and the rest of the group, **Zak**, a street performer by trade, hesitantly agrees to tell the group the truth about his relationship with **Jason** as an animated performed fairy tale, featuring Prince Jason, King (Curtis and Jason's biological father), Queen (Curtis and Jason's mother) and New King (their stepdad). **Zak**'s story reveals to **Curtis** that his family were complicit in his brother's disappearance.

Zak   The King's death sent the Queen mad. She started to bring wolves into the castle. She cried, 'My precious wolves. They are all I need.'

[…]

Prince Jason couldn't bear to see the Queen so distressed. He went on long walks. He walked to parts of the Kingdom he'd never been to before. One day he found himself by the edge of a – oh my!

[…]

It's a lagoon. The water is smooth as glass and blue as cornflowers. […] The Prince sits beside it. A young man comes up and sits beside the Prince and says, 'You know, there's a legend about this lagoon. It says that dolphins will appear whenever two people who are in love with each other are reflected in the water.' […] He's called … Spiral. Prince Jason and Spiral sit by the edge of the lagoon and talk. They talk all day and into the night. They talk like they have never talked to anyone before. Like they've known each other all their lives. Then they hold each other. Then they kiss each other. They look at their reflections on the surface of the lagoon. And … dolphins appear.

Slight pause.

Back to the Queen!

[…]

The Queen has met a New King now. The Queen is in love with this New King. They plan to get married. […] But there's a problem.

[…]

The lagoon. Moonlight. Stars. Prince Jason says to Spiral, 'I've never felt like this towards … another boy. You've made me feel lots of new things. Up until now my life has been in neat boxes. All of them ordered and labelled. But you … you have come along and blown all the boxes apart. I want us to get as close as possible in all possible ways.' And Spiral says, 'I feel the same.

That's why I have made you a gift to celebrate what we have created together …'

[…]

'Once a month the dolphins collect moonlight from the surface of the lagoon. This moonlight is the most precious thing in the whole world. I have woven it into this garment, my Prince. See how it sparkles. Please put it on … It is called Moonfleece!'

[…]

The New King says to the Queen, 'There must be a reason why our lives went so wrong.' The Queen says, 'I agree, but what could it have been?' The New King says, 'Well, my wife died when the moon was full.' The Queen says, 'I think the moon was full when my husband was killed too.' The New King says, 'That's it! Don't you see? The moon is to blame for everything.' The Queen says, 'Goodness, I've been so blind.' The New King says, 'We'll create a new kingdom without anything to do with the moon! People who like the moon will be banished. All references to the moon will be taken out of the books. If the moon shines at night people must close their windows. If they happen to catch sight of it they must abuse it. And we will name this new kingdom after me. We will call it Avalon!' – you see the problem, sweet Apprentice?

[…]

Ahhhhh!

[…]

I'm the Queen. […] I've just seen Prince Jason. […] 'What are you wearing, my son?' 'Moonfleece.' 'Moon! Haven't you heard anything King Avalon has been saying?' 'That's crazy talk, Mum.' 'Shhh! King Avalon will hear you.' 'Too late, my love. I heard everything!' 'I'm sure he didn't mean it.' 'I do, Mum!' 'Take it off, Jason!' 'No, Avalon! I like it!' 'It's disgusting!' 'It's not!' 'Then you can't be part of this new family.' 'Please, son. Do it for me!' 'I'd do anything for you, Mum! You know I would! But I must wear Moonfleece! Moonfleece is what I am!' 'Listen, you pervert! I have ambitions! Plans for my future kingdom are taking shape. Someone like you could ruin everything for me. I can't have you around. I will give you a chest of gold to start a new life elsewhere. We will tell everyone here that you were killed in an accident. A fatal accident. I will fake all the necessary documents. You will never show your face in this kingdom again. You must never make contact with your mum. Or your younger brother.'

[…]

Prince Jason has a younger brother. Ain't I mentioned that? What a bloody oversight. His name's Prince Curtis. And Prince Curtis adores Prince Jason. You remember when their real Dad – the old King – had been killed? Prince Jason looked took care of Prince Curtis after that. And now their new Dad, this Avalon, is telling Jason he must go away and never see his Mum or Curtis again. And Jason says, 'If that's what my Mum wants, I'll do it. But only if it's what *she* wants. Do you want me to disappear, Mum? Do you?'

[…] 'Yes.'

From

OFF THE ENDZ

by Bola Agbaje

Off the Endz premiered at the Royal Court Jerwood Theatre
Downstairs, Sloane Square in London on 11 February 2010. This
production was directed by Jeremy Herrin with the following cast:
Ashley Walters (David), Lorraine Burroughs (Sharon), Madeline
Appiah (Keisha), Daniel Francis (Kojo), Natasha Williams
(Marsha) and Brandon Benoit-Joyce, Omar Brown, Thomas
Eghator, René Gray (Boys).

Bola Agbaje's play explores the barriers that prevent people from
climbing the social ladder, owning their homes and moving 'off
the endz'. Set on a London council estate during the recession,
Off the Endz juxtaposes the lives of three characters –David, an
ex-prisoner, and Kojo and Sharon, a young, educated, hardworking,
pregnant couple – who all dream of a better life. But with limited
means to turn their pipe dreams into a reality, will they be able
to resist participating in the fast-money dodgy dealings that exist
within the estate walls? *Off the Endz* is a gripping drama about
morals, ambition, rehabilitation and second chances.

The play opens in Kojo and Sharon's modern-day, well-kitted-out
council flat. David, newly released from prison, arrives at their
front door, looking very scruffy with a bruised, swollen eye and
a cut lip. His arrival can only mean trouble. In the absence of
best friend Kojo, opportunist David makes sexual advances to
his friend's pregnant girlfriend, refusing to let Sharon forget their
past fling. But things have changed drastically since David's
imprisonment. With a baby on the way and their sights on a three-
bedroom house in Sydenham, nurse Sharon takes pleasure in
informing David of her and corporate suit-wearing Kojo's plans to
set up a family home far away from the endz. David has nowhere
to go and Sharon takes pity on her injured long-time friend and
agrees to let him live back in their home in the interim.

David is eager to catch up with best chum Kojo to proposition him
about a drug-dealing quick-money scheme. Kojo initially declines.

As the play develops, the cracks in the couple's dreams are exposed. Kojo is holding on to his job by a thread and unbeknown to his partner Sharon, his salary is still not enough to clear the debt from credit cards and store cards as well as their daily bills. Kojo has had no choice but to dip into the couple's deposit fund for the house and, to make matters worse, his workplace has gone into administration, leaving Kojo without a job.

With David's offer still on the table, Kojo has to decide whether to disappoint the woman he loves by coming clean about their financial predicament or to partner with David in selling hard drugs for quick money and freedom from debt.

Summary (extract)

Twenty-six-year-old **David** is a confident chauvinist, who never backs down from a fight, but is always ready for an easy way to make money. He has recently been released from prison and already has his mind set on making fast money illegally with the help of **Kojo**. Now all he has to do is persuade his best friend.

David   I want to start my own small business. [...] Yeah man.
[...] I've been thinking bout it for a while ... When I was back
in the pen and dat, bare mans were on different movement and
they were all willing to bring me in. But I wanted something for
myself, you feel me? Anyway, some of the tings that some of them
were on about they were making proper peas from it. I mean,
some mans were making serious dough ... So I was thinking
proper hard, looking for an investor. Someone who knows me
and I know them ... and it hit me, who better for me to go into
business with – than you ... You're my boy ... family. We been
thru a lot and if a woman couldn't come between us then ... boy,
money can't. You feel me, and seeing as you are having all them
problems at work, once we got this started you can tell your boss
to lick your balls.

*He searches his pockets for a crumpled piece of paper. He opens it
out and hands it to* **Kojo**. **David** *laughs to himself as* **Kojo** *begins
reading it.* **Kojo** *is stunned.*

Don't do your face like that. It's a popular product, like alcohol
or cigarettes. People love those products and not cos they wanna
kill themselves. They can't help but love them. They're addictive.
That's what we need – an addictive product. We need to follow
their formula. Can't fail.

[...]

See the bigger picture. You will be investing in an empire. [...]
I'm being real fam! Look, I have even worked out the maths for
you. If you invest five grand I'd use that as my start-up capital.
I will flip that five grand in a month. I'll get five z's of the shine
and I'll pick up every week. At the end of the month I'd have
bout nine grand, give or take, and we can halve the profit. I'll take
my two grand, reinvest it. You gets your five grand back plus the
two grand profit. You would have seven grand. What bank do you
know would give you a quick return like that on your money?

[...]

Blud, we can't go wrong.

From

SOUTHBRIDGE

by Reginald Edmund

Southbridge was produced by Chicago Dramatists, Chicago, Illinois, on 24 January 2013, directed by Russ Tutterow, with the following cast: Manny Buckley (Christopher), Gene Cordon (Local Sheriff), Ashley Elizabeth Honore (Nadia), Wendy Robie (Lucinda Luckey) and Lance Newton (Edwin Berry).

Chicago-based (originally from Houston, Texas) playwright Reginald Edmund unearths a hidden and deeply tragic historical event that happened in Athens, Ohio, in 1881: the lynching of Christopher W. Davis. On the night of 21 November 1881, a 'mulatto' man was jailed for a shocking assault on an elderly white widow, Lucinda Luckey, who allegedly was subjected to rape and violently beaten over the head with an axe, fracturing her skull and leaving her for dead. Miraculously she recovered consciousness by morning and managed to crawl to the house of a neighbour to inform them of the horrific incident. Christopher W. Davis was held in jail and confronted by an angry mob who broke into his cell and bribed him to confess to the crime, assuring him that if he agreed they would not hang him. After being reassured for the second time, he confessed 'I am the man'. A rope was tied to the bridge, with a noose around his neck, which was broken by the fall.

Reginald Edmund's play *Southbridge* is a fictional story detailing the events leading to the lynching of Christopher W. Davis. Set in the autumn of 1881 in the township of Athens, Ohio, Edmund reimagines the relationship between Christopher (also known as Stranger) and Lucinda as a consensual sexual affair. The story jumps from Christopher's imprisonment to flashbacks depicting the blossoming of his relationship with widow Lucinda Luckey. At the start of the play, we hear an angry mob in the near distance as the imprisoned lead character Christopher reasserts his innocence to the devious local Sheriff (known as Ward), which falls on deaf ears.

A flashback to Christopher with his best and only friend Edwin
Berry, a successful, shrewd businessman whose ruthless,
underhanded dealings have earned him the title of being
untrustworthy is shown. Edwin has convinced Christopher to
partner, with him in his prospective hotel business and has devised
a way for Christopher to come up with the required financial
deposit. Christopher is a bricklayer by trade with the ability to
see visions, a talent which has earned him the name 'Stranger'
and made him the most feared person in the community, whose
members view his gift as an act of the devil. It has been rumoured
that Christopher caused the death of a baby who died three days
after being held by him, a tale which has ruined the chances of
the love of his life, African American wife, Nadia, pursuing her
much-loved teaching career. From one outcast to another, Edwin
has masterfully arranged for his future business partner to meet
with Lucinda, a lonely widow who has gained a reputation as a
mean-spirited woman ever since her father passed away. Lucinda
is looking for a worker and is more than happy to accept help
from the charming Christopher.

But when Sheriff Ward discovers that Lucinda has hired
Christopher for home repairs and gardening, he cannot hide
his resentment. Ward has been trying in vain to win the
affections of Lucinda since he was a young lad. When he finds
out about their love affair he uses this information to help exact a
terrible revenge.

Summary (extract)

In the evening at **Lucinda**'s house, **Christopher** (a twenty-
three-year-old African American man) and **Lucinda** (a
fifty-five-year-old white American woman) are putting their
clothes back on. She notices the scars on his back which resemble
the tree over the Southbridge. **Christopher** is keen to return to
his wife, but **Lucinda** does not want him to leave. In an attempt
to make him stay longer, she begs for Christopher to explain the
marks on his back and his ability to see visions. **Christopher**
reluctantly tells his story.

Christopher   I was in the farm house stable working as a child,
when an old woman came in hummin' ... looked at me. Waved
me on over to follow her. And I did, don't know why, just did. I
still remember that old woman, see her in my dreams. She had a
look on her face. Her eyes, I ain't ever seen eyes like that. Seemed
like every drop of tears in that old woman's body had been wept
outta her. She took my little hand and guided me on down to
this clearing at the end of the property to an old ash tree. Old
and twisted from time and there I saw a man legs just danglin'.
His hands tied behind his back. And flies fat from feedin' off his
misery circled him. I looked up into his vacant eyes and they
looked back at me. Accusing me. I wanted to run, wanted to leave
that place and not look back but I couldn't ... My feet was rooted
to the earth ... After a moment I found that the man swinging by
the neck ... Had disappeared. Faded away into the afternoon sun.
When I looked around saw the same with the old woman too.
Gone ... I found myself standing there still in that stable. I had
never left, but something was different about me. Had these scar
upon my back, marking me for life. Every morning I wake up to
find a new scar upon me. But I could feel something else as well
... This pressure as if a rope was tightening around my neck. And
I was struggling to breathe. Feel it everyday I wake up. Feel it
every time I walk down these streets. Feel it every time I look into
someone's eyes. Like I was being strangled by something I can't
see. Something I can never cut loose.

From

THE ELABORATE ENTRANCE OF CHAD DEITY

by Kristoffer Diaz

The Elaborate Entrance of Chad Deity was first produced by the
Victory Gardens Theater in Chicago, Illinois, on 25 September
2009. The performance was directed by Edward Torres, with
the following cast: Usman Ally (Vigneshwar Paduar also known
as VP), Kamal Angelo Bolden (Chad Deity), Desmin Borges
(Macedonio Guerra also known as Mace), James Krag (Everett K.
Olson also known as EKO/Ring Announcer) and Christian Litke
(Joe Jabroni/Bill Heartland/Old Glory).

The play was subsequently produced by Second Stage Theatre
in New York City on 20 May 2010, directed by Edward Torres,
with the following cast: Usman Ally (Vigneshwar Paduar),
Terrence Archie (Chad Deity), Desmin Borges (Macedonio
Guerra), Michael T. Weiss (Everett K. Olson/Ring Announcer) and
Christian Litke (Joe Jabroni/Bill Heartland/Old Glory).

The multi-award-winning play *The Elaborate Entrance of Chad
Deity* by American playwright Kristoffer Diaz is a thought-
provoking dramatic comedy about wrestling, geopolitics and
racial stereotypes. Although the title refers to the character Chad
Deity, this is Macedonio Guerra's (aka Mace) story. Mace is a
Bronxite Puerto Rican whose deep obsession with wrestling as
a child surpassed that of his brothers. He secures his childhood
dream to become a professional wrestler at THE Wrestling, the
largest wrestling organization in the world, owned by the highly
respected Everett K. Olson (known simply as EKO). There is no
denying that Mace is a really good wrestler but that is more reason
for him to take on the job as the loser, hired to make the cash
cow Chad Deity look good. The African American champion of
THE Wrestling, Chad Deity, is not a very good wrestler, but he
has all the winning components to fulfil the role of a megastar:
good looks, popularity, confidence, jewellery, as well as the ability
to sell tickets and merchandise. The character of Chad Deity is
manufactured to comply with the black male stereotype – hip hop

music plays as he enters the arena, he is strong, huge, obnoxious and all about the flashing lights and money (sporting the big gold champion belt), epitomizing the American Dream.

But when Mace spots a young, tall, lanky Indian-American Brooklynite who calls himself VP (Vigneshwar Paduar), he is convinced that this kid can change wrestling and the face of multiculturalism forever. Skilled basketballer VP has perfected trash talking in many different languages (Spanish, English, Hindu, Urdu, Polish, Italian and even Japanese) – a natural smooth operator with the ladies and an articulate outspoken entertainer, set to rival the seemingly untouchable Chad Deity, is in search of a stage and audience. Mace decides to get him a job at THE Wrestling. EKO spots an opportunity for a sellable duo act, Mace and VP, offering them the role of terrorists.

Summary (extract)

EKO has had a lightbulb moment and shares his idea for **VP** to play the role of a cave-dwelling Muslim fundamentalist, a sellable addition to THE Wrestling that will definitely incite hatred towards the Mulims characters and increase **Chad Deity**'s popularity. **Mace** tries desperately to overturn **EKO**'s decision, but **EKO** fails to see a place in the market for a Spanish-speaking Indian-American wrestler. After much deliberation and to **Mace**'s astonishment, **VP** agrees to take on the role, with **Mace** reluctantly following suit as Che Chavez Castro, the Mexican revolutionary. The show has begun. **Chad Deity** speaks to the crowd, sympathizing with their need for the American Dream by using the metaphor of raisin bread, insinuating that he can give them what they want, unlike the duo who can only provide them with bread. Before the reaction from the duo, **EKO** speaks on behalf of THE Wrestling to address the television audience to disown the views about to be stated by the controversial wrestlers. **Mace** and **VP** take to the stage. **Mace** has one phrase that he repeats in an angry tone: 'CHAD DEITY', as **VP** delivers a speech that threatens to damage Chad Deity's reputation forever.

VP   Every five, six seconds or so, Mace drops that name, and every time he spits that name, the name of the champion of the world, all I do is smirk.

Every time that name shoots out of Mace's mouth, my mind races to raisin bread, and that takes care of the smirk – couldn't hold my ridicule in if I tried. And I got exactly zero interest in trying.

We got a Black world champion and he's rich and he God Blesses America, and he talks vociferous and he's non-threatening unless you yourself are a threat to that which he God Blesses, and you ain't a threat because you're physically imposing or because you might pull off your fucking dashiki – or whatever the fuck you terrorist types wear – and bomb an arena full of God-fearing, Chad Deity-fearing, tax-paying, ticket-buying Americans, but you're a threat because Chad Deity drew a fucking line in the sand and instead of stepping over that line so Chad Deity could pick you up, powerbomb you, pin you, you held your ground and didn't speak and dared that dude to meet you on your side of his stupid fucking line of fiction.

And my Indian ass stands right here next to my Puerto Rican brother, Macedonio Guerra, and every time that names shoots out of his mouth, I can feel him drifting back to The Bronx while it was burning and being told to drop dead, drifting back to Vieques and mandated sterilization and a commonwealth government without the money to keep itself in business and illegal occupations, and extraordinary rendition, and fuck that – right now a nation full of 'patriots' who love to complain about how fucked up everything is, but ain't willing to sacrifice a goddamn thing for the benefit of the greater good – and Chad Deity's still out here God Blessing America. And yeah, wrestling don't got nothing to do with politics, and Chad Deity ain't the reason that what's wrong is wrong, but for someone who represents everything that's supposed to be right, that motherfucker ain't yet gave me one reason to respect him.

From

TRUE BRITS

by Vinay Patel

True Brits was produced by Rich Mason Productions in
association with HighTide Festival and had its premiere at
Assembly Hall, Edinburgh on 31 July 2014. This production was
directed by Tanith Lindon and performed by Sid Sagar.

South-east London playwright Vinay Patel's sharp, witty and
brutally honest one-man play explores the challenging question:
'Can a South Asian person ever be classified as a True Brit?' The
play tells the story of British South Asian Rahul, who questions
his patriotism when he notices only two Asians out of over 500
athletes in the Great British team at the 2012 London Olympics, a
world event which was considered the golden moment of diversity
and inclusion. His story flashes back to 2005 to show personal
and key events exposing social attitudes towards the South
Asian Muslim community before and after the 7/7 bus and train
bombings in London. Covering themes of interracial relationships,
activism, patriotism and racism, *True Brits* forces us to re-examine
our attitudes to identity, Britishness and nationalism.

Twenty-five-year-old non-devout Muslim Rahul was born and
raised in Bexleyheath, a suburban district in south-east London,
unlike his Indian grandfather who sacrificed everything to come to
London to be British. While his grandfather proudly worships all
things British, his mum on the contrary, is convinced that they still
don't belong in London, leaving Rahul in the middle questioning
his allegiance to his homeland. A flashback to 2005 introduces us
to Rahul aged eighteen; it's his birthday and the same day as the
Iraqi War protest march. Activist Jess, his white girlfriend and
daughter of the local councillor and head of racial equality, Mr
Collins, violently protests holding a banner marked 'True Brits 4
Peace', as well as taking pride in learning Arabic. Despite being
beaten up by a gang of boys for looking at Jess after the protest,
Rahul is determined to prove his mother wrong. But after the
7/7 terrorist attacks, his fight to remain a part of British society

that has grown to despise him becomes more difficult. Paranoia and mistrust sweeps the nation; despite Rahul following his mum's advice by shaving his beard, he is watched and scrutinized by everyone, including Mr Collins and Jess. Targeted random searches are carried out under the Prevention of Terrorism Act 2005 in an effort to make the public feel safe, resulting in the killing of an unarmed Brazilian, who was shot in the head by the police.

As Rahul is pushed further away from the centre of British society, he meets Mihir, a protester against the brutality, targeting and violence of the Muslim community post-7/7. Mihir metaphorically holds up a mirror to Rahul's life, forcing Rahul to realize that he is fighting the wrong fight and questioning Rahul's loyalty to his Muslim community. This all is too much for Rahul to digest and he violently attacks Mihir, resulting in his imprisonment.

In prison, a man breaks all the fingers in Rahul's right hand. But the year spent in prison is not all bad for Rahul, who learns Arabic with the help of a Lebanese jail-mate and is left holding Jess's hand.

Summary (extract)

Flashback to early August 2005 during the aftermath of the 7/7 attacks. Eighteen-year-old boisterous **Rahul** speaks with an estuary accent as he travels on the bus to his girlfriend's family home for dinner. He holds a bunch of flowers for his girlfriend in his hands.

Rahul   See-through backpacks – a sign of cowardice, an admission of guilt, or just a plain old fashion disaster? Seen them about in the last couple of weeks, and I can't decide.

The sight of the park and the stench of piss on the bus combine to hit me with an unexpected wave of nostalgia. It may be a shithole, but it's my shithole and I know I'm gonna miss all this when I'm at uni. A kid gets on and sees me, sees the flowers in my hands and screws his little face up.

'Who are those for?'

'My girlfriend.' It's fun to say that.

'Does she like flowers?'

Hadn't actually considered that. But everyone likes flowers.

'Course. Everyone likes flowers, so I'm giving her flowers.'

'Why? Did you try to blow her up?'

Woah. I mean, I laugh, I do laugh, I like a dark joke as much as anyone, but tell him that it might be a bit soon. He makes a face and goes back to what I think passes for a Game Boy these days.

When I ring the bell to get off, the boy starts to sing, and he's got this sweet soprano voice …

To the tune of 'If You're Happy and You Know It'.

If you're a Paki and unhappy, fuck off home.
If you're a Paki and unhappy, fuck off home.
If you're a Paki and unhappy and you wanna go jihadi,
Just fuck off little Paki, fuck off home.

No one says anything. You don't do you, on a bus?

If not quite 'The Universal' but it's actually sort of catchy. I find myself singing it as I knock on Jess's door but stop myself when she opens it. She's had a hair cut. And she looks. Thinner. A lot thinner.

As expected, she's got three As. Two Bs and an A for me but it's enough. Dinner with 'the in-laws' is always a bit awkward, but no problem this time, 'cause Jess is back to her old self, doesn't let anyone get a word in edgeways. She's excited about uni, about a future of possibilities, and as we get through starters – if you call a stick of Sainsbury's garlic bread starters – her dad just lets her run on and on, his face stupid with pride and I'm glad we're all doing OK.

Jess pushes her plate away, hardly eaten a thing, and says she's going to get some water, leaving me alone with the MegaBeard. Fuck.

'You see the second Test, Clive?' Expression noted. Don't call him Clive.

'Not been following it this year.'

'Oh you should, it's been epic. Scraped it by two runs!'

Clive cuts at his carrots.

'How about the Olympics, you excited about the Olympics? Imagine the borough'll go big for it.'

'That's all a long way off. Way the world's going, we might not even get there.'

'I nod and put fully half a pie into my face.

'Are you a Muslim, Rahul?' Pastry flakes from my mouth.

'H-hey?'

'Muslim. Yes? No?'

'I, um … well … why are you asking?'

'Are you?'

'It doesn't really matter, does it?'

'You are then.'

'Would you prefer it if I was, or if I wasn't?'

'I don't have a preference, of course I don't. I was just curious is all, you seem a bit evasive about it.'

'Not trying to be evasive, Mr C.'

'But trying to make a point?'

'No point, never a point, an eternal broken pencil, me.'

'Well, it's a pork pie we're having here, so … thought I'd check!'

He snorts out a laugh and dives back into his veggies.

'You can eat with your hands, if it'd make you more comfortable.'

The rest of dinner is torture and when I get in the car I let Mum know that for once I'm grateful for the lift. She tosses me a see-through backpack.

'What the fuck is this?'

She belts me proper hard.

Apparently the windows at the shop have been spray painted with something obscene. And Mihir's told her about some Asian kid, a Sikh, getting beaten up, five guys, forty-three stitches.

'See!' She says, starting up the engine. 'You can be friends with the whites, but when it comes down to it, the only ones who'll really care for you when it gets rough is us, our people.'

She's been waiting to say that for years.

'Spray paint's not exactly a brick, Mum, and people get attacked all the time, it doesn't necessarily – I mean, who's to know? Not Muhir, he's fucking simple!'

She smacks me again.

'He wasn't even one of them!' She's not listening to a word I've said.

'Hey, maybe you'd be happier in India, Mum, back in Gujarat, I mean they only have murderous riots over there, much better than a couple of beatings.'

We're in Britain, we should reset. I mean you don't hear the Royal Family banging on about their German roots, do you? They don't invite you to the Palace garden for tea and bratwurst.

Mum's a coward and she can go wherever she wants.

Me? I'm sticking around, I'm making it work.

I'm the reset button.

From

SNOOKERED

by Ishy Din

Snookered was produced by Tamasha Theatre Company in association with Oldham Coliseum Theatre and Bush Theatre. The play received its world premiere at Oldham Coliseum Theatre at the Oldham University Campus on 2 February 2012, followed by a national tour. The production was directed by Iqbal Khan with the following cast: Muzz Khan (Shaf), Jaz Deol (Billy), Asif Khan (Kamy), Peter Singh (Mo) and Michael Luxton (Dave).

From a taxi driver to promising playwright, Ishy Din stormed onto the theatre scene with his debut play *Snookered*. Set in a northern snooker hall, Din's hard-hitting, witty and unapologetically provocative play explores the lives of four young British Muslim men trapped between two different cultures. Each character struggles to carry out his cultural duties and traditions whilst trying to fit into British society and fulfil their own personal aspirations. *Snookered* is a story about dreams, guilt, disappointments and values.

Four young men in their twenties reunite to commemorate the sixth anniversary of the death of their school-friend Talub Hussein (known as T). As they trickle into a dingy snooker hall, hot-headed, vulgar-mouthed taxi driver Shaf is ready for a night of heavy drinking, sexual banter and the possible occasional fight. Shaf cares the least about honouring his friend T's death; he is more enthusiastic about the prospect of seeing his good friend Billy to offer him a life-changing proposition which could give Shaf, a father of four with another on the way, the break that he has always been looking for. Estranged friend Billy has returned from London to see his old friends, but has no intention of visiting his family who disowned him for dating outside of his race. Eager-to-please outsider of the group, Kamy, is keen to play snooker so that he can show off his cherished gift, a 'lucky' cue stick from deceased friend T, which he believes will help him win the game as well as the long-awaited respect and acceptance from his former school mates.

As the boys gather, Shaf does his best to mask his avoidance of numerous calls to his mobile; turning his phone on and off, he claims that it is playing up and refuses to allow Kamy to fix it.

Shaf struggles to find the optimum moment to disclose his undercover dodgy business plans with best chum Billy away from the prying presence of Kamy. Like any reunion, the conversation gradually centres on work, with Billy's anticipated promotion at his workplace and underdog Kamy's business plans to expand his dad's family business with aspirations to succeed his father; uninspired and frustrated by his mundane long-standing job as a taxi driver, Shaf has nothing to feed back to the group. His insecurities play out through his aggressive drinking and once again he reverts to being the school bully, violently forcing his peers to participate in his drinking binge.

A visit from Shaf's rival, his brother in-law Mo, rehashes past resentments. To make matters worse, Mo is paired with Billy for the snooker game and the two create a natural kinship and win the game. Fuelled by jealousy, alcohol and bitterness, Shaf is tipped even further over the edge; unable to control his emotions he attempts to shame Mo. But when this backfires, he is left with no option but to get one over on Mo by revealing a hidden secret, which triggers a stint of confessions as the night catastrophically crashes to a halt.

Summary (extract)

Set in an unnamed northern town, belligerent **Shaf** (a British-Pakistani taxi driver in his early twenties) attempts to entertain his former school buddies by bragging about his visit to the pub to watch the England game which ended in a fight.

Shaf   So anyway I'm watching the game and having a craic with these two ghoray, and at half time one of them says to me … he says, 'The problem with you Asians is that you don't integrate.'

[…]

Fucking right he meant Pakis.

[…]

When your average white man says Asian he means … Paki.

[…]

So this fucker says to me, he says, 'You Pakis don't integrate' … and I say to him, I say, ''ere mate I'm stood in a pub, drinking a pint, watching England play football, what more do you want me to do, get a fucking Union Jack tattooed across my cock?'

The other two find this hilarious.

[…]

They fucking jumped me.

[…]

I go for a piss and I'm stood there and I hear the door open, I look over my shoulder and it's only Nick Griffin and his pal, so I know what's coming. I wait until I think he's in striking distance and I turn and bang! I drop him like a toilet seat, good fucking night Vienna, his mate only swings at me with a bottle, a fucking Bud thank you very much, but I'm bobbing and weaving and he misses and I'm like bish bosh and he's fucking down as well. So I'm stood over them, cock still out, piss all over the place and I'm giving it the big COME ON THEN! LET'S FUCKING GO! LET'S FUCKING DO IT! The barman only walks in, thinks I'm doing a George Michael and bars me out, the cunt.

[…]

I pissed on them … I forced all the piss I had left out and I pissed on them … no fucking white bastard […] calls me a Paki and gets away with it.

From

THE EMPIRE

by DC Moore

The Empire premiered at the Jerwood Theatre Upstairs of
the Royal Court Theatre in London on 31 March 2010. This
production was directed by Mike Bradwell, with the following
cast: Nav Sidhu (Zia), Josef Altin (Hafizullah), Joe Armstrong
(Gary), Rufus Wright (Captain Simon Mannock) and Imran Khan
(Jalander). The production was critically acclaimed, winning the
2010 TMA Award for best touring production and nominated for
a 2010 Olivier Award for Outstanding Achievement in Affiliated
Theatre. DC Moore was nominated for the Evening Standard
Award for Most Promising Playwright based on this play.

British playwright DC Moore's witty drama is set during the war
in Afghanistan. Moore uses both British and Afghan characters to
explore how colonialism, racism and nationalism exist in twenty-
first-century war zones. Inspired by Sean Langan's documentaries
about British soldiers in Afghanistan, *The Empire* is less
concerned about tackling the politics of war, but more interested in
delving deeper into the of the minds of soldiers who are placed in
pressurized situations and expected to make life-or-death decisions
based mainly on their values and moral standing. When the person
in question for an attack is revealed as a British man, the British
soldiers are faced with an unexpected dilemma. This provocative
play deliberately ends on a cliffhanger, with no resolution or clear
indication of right or wrong – and furthermore, what the truth
actually is.

The action takes place in an empty room which is part of
an abandoned compound in the remote Helmand Province
of Afghanistan in the summer of 2006. In the absence of
Commanding Officer Simon Mannock – who is busy organizing
medical aid for one his soldiers, Phipps, who was badly wounded
by a rocket-propelled grenade attack – British soldier Gary and
his new-found assistant, Afghan National Army soldier Hafizullah
(whom he renames Paddy) guard an injured prisoner and the

suspected perpetrator of the attack. Although the injured prisoner seems to be dead, covered from head to toe in a sheet, the soldiers have been ordered to wait for the medics to treat his injuries before turning him over to the Afghan National Army, who are eagerly waiting to kill him.

The situation immediately becomes surprisingly complicated when the prisoner, Zia, wakes up in pain from a broken leg, reaffirming his innocence by telling the soldiers that he is not a part of the Taliban. Zia, a British citizen from Newham in London, goes on to explain that there has been a big mistake, claiming that an innocent trip to visit his family in Lahore with his uncle ended up with him reluctantly accompanying his uncle's friend, a business associate, to Afghanistan to get more supplies. This resulted in him being kidnapped by the Taliban and forced into the centre of the battle.

Being a fellow Brit from an area not far from Zia's home, Gary is initially taken by Zia's story and is ready to follow the commander's suggestion of sending the injured prisoner by helicopter to Camp Bastion. But when he learns that his close friend Phipps is dying from his injuries, he lashes out violently against Zia, standing on the thigh of his broken leg whilst threatening to kill him. Captain Simon steps in to diffuse the situation. But when the helicopter arrives, Simon, Gary and Hafizullah remain indecisive of their next move.

Summary (extract)

Zia, a British-Asian man from Newham, East London, has a healthy beard, a broken leg, and his hands are bound by plasticuffs. He opens his eyes to see the soldiers standing around his body, feeling immense pain from his injury. **Gary** accuses him of trying to kill him and his comrades. **Zia** responds by laughing nervously. Struggling to find the best way to explain himself, he tries to convince **Gary** that he is a good, innocent guy on holiday.

Zia   I told you. I'm telling you. Thank you. Thank you, mate.
Thank you. (*Pause.*) I'm on holiday. I'm on. And it wasn't like
a piss-up or nothing – I don't drink or do none of that, yeah?
Though I used to, back in the day, I was a bit of a boy, yeah? But,
but not now though, no way, cut it all out, started going to the
gym, all this, proper detox, like my body is … now, I'm like …
So yeah, it was just meant to be like a quiet family holiday thing
this time. Went to Pakistan first and I just came over with some,
some business. […] No, no, just let me talk, yeah? Explain this
to you. Honestly. […] Where you getting that? I didn't have no
[AK-forty] […] I don't know *nothing* about […]. I mean, it might
have been in the general, like, area but it weren't … mine. […] It
musta, yeah, belonged to the guys who like. Kidnapped me. […]
One of them. […] By … by the guys you must be […] like. […]
Fighting. Yeah.

Zia *nods.*

That's what happened bruv. […] Look. […] I can understand –
totally – if you don't like, believe that. […] Cos I know it don't
look good from where you're standing, from what you … from
all what you're saying. But what I'm trying to do, is tell you. The
truth. […] I'm … Yeah. I'm trying to but you keep … fucking …
[…] Like. Interrupting. […] Yes. It's quite. Annoying actually.
OK. […] OK. Thank you. It just all got a bit. Much. […]

Holiday. […] OK. OK. I was. I was with my uncle in Lahore,
yeah? For the holiday. Just like a family thing. Just visiting for a
few weeks, like on the break from college. And, and I was a bit
[…] No. No. I was a bit lonely, to be honest with you. Not in a
gay way. I just. Missed it. […] England. Home. […]

Pause.

Everything, bruv. Pakistan is so … like. Everything. Decent cars.
Decent TV. Decent. Women. All of it, you know? Something
to do. Anything. You don't realize till you go. What you. Miss.
[…] Yeah. (*Pause.*) And my uncle's bit of a. Dick. Like he's a
proper. Total. And my auntie she *talks* like. *Constantly*. About.
Nothing. I mean she could, she could talk to you for three hours

nonstop about her *shoes* or something, I swear that. Like, I think she literally did that first day I got there. Just sat me down in the kitchen and talked and talked and talked and *then* showed me so many fucking photos you would not believe that. They've just got this like this digital camera thing – fuck me, yeah? – and they will take like a picture of every single family person in every single room in every single possible combination of all those people – you know what family are like yeah? – and they will then show you every single one of them they take in order and talk you through the whole fucking thing and you have to visibly show that you are very interested by *all of them*. […] And I musta seen like … And all this. So I was thinking about coming home early anyways, but then […] I thought … I thought you said you wouldn't like. Interrupt. […]

Anyway, moving on yeah. Then. Then, after a few days of that, my uncle's … my uncle's friend. This business associate. He comes over to their house, visiting as part of his business, and he's this fucked-up, crazy Afghan guy yeah? […] Mohammed. […] Mohammed Qasim. And him and my uncle got this tidy little profit hing going on, yeah? Like he's bringing all these like all these textiles over from Kabul. […] Yeah, and they're using them in my uncle's massive, like, factory in Lahore and making plenty of cash, bruv. And this guy, this guy, he's like – Mohammed Qasim – proper *crazy*. He's always laughing and joking and smiling and he's got this *energy* you know when he comes into the room and we get on *like this immediately* – fucking … sparks – he speaks well good English which is great because my Urdu is a bit fucked up, a bit rusty to be honest with you and I probably speak less Pashtu than you, yeah? […] And he says to me. Mohammed Qasim says to me – I'm getting there, alright? OK? I'm getting there, soon, hold on, hold up bruv – after we've been chatting bare shit for ages, he says: 'I like you. I like you, Zia, very much. We got a connection. So. You. Me. You, you come to Afghanistan with me. I'm going back for more supplies. I'll be two weeks at the most and you will see the most beautiful things and the most beautiful people in the whole world.' […] And I was all like: 'Fuck that, yeah?' I was polite, though, I didn't actually swear when I actually said it – like he's a friend of the family, you know what I'm saying? – but I was all like: 'Thank you very much, that is a brilliant offer, thank you so much for that, but I can't do that, yeah? I would love to, yeah, but that is way too dangerous for me. There's a war there, you know what I'm saying?' But he was all like: 'No no no, Zia, with me, with me you will be safe. There will be no problems with me. I know all the people, I am loved and known by all the people. So if you say: "No", you're disrespecting *me*, my family, my country and *my honour as a Muslim*.' (*Pause*.) So I'm like: ... Like: 'OK. Yeah. If ... I will then. Thank you.' Even though I really didn't want to. And then. [...] And then ... [...] we ... we ... and *then* [...] Look. I'm not a ... a 'gangsta'. [...] And I'm not saying generally I'm like. Mother Theresa or ... I done a little bit of fucked-up shit like everyone I know yeah? Like I'm sure you done. But, I didn't try to kill no one. That is not ... I'm not ... I was ... I was *kidnapped* and and I ... I don't know how else to tell you this. I mean, do I look like a fucking ...? [...] But I'm ... I'm in the middle here, mate. That is all it is. I got caught up, bruv. Just, *trust me* on that. I swear to you. I just wanna ... I just wanna go home.

From

THE FEVER CHART

Three Visions of the Middle East

by Naomi Wallace

The Fever Chart: Three Visions of the Middle East was produced
in 2008 at New York's Public Theater as part of the Public
Lab series. It was directed by Jo Bonney, with the following
cast: *Vision One: A State of Innocence*: Lameece Issaq (Um
Hisham Qishta), Arian Moayed (Yuval) and Waleed F. Zuaiter
(Shlomo). *Vision Two: Between This Breath and You*: Waleed F.
Zuaiter (Mourid Kamal), Natalie Gold (Tanya Langer) and Arian
Moayed (Sami Elbaz). *Vision Three: The Retreating World*: Omar
Metwally (Ali).

Naomi Wallace's trilogy of short, provocative and deeply moving
plays about loss is set in various locations in the Middle East. *The
Fever Chart* comprises three stand-alone stories all based on real
experiences, portraying a snapshot of some of the most difficult
and harrowing events, including being forced to face enemies
and even death itself. Each vision (play) is kept minimalistic with
a bare stage and a few simple hard chairs; the events play out
effortlessly, with no resolution, the same way as life itself. Like
the characters on the stage, the audience are helpless, incapable of
finding solutions to the ever-growing harsh realities of living in a
war-torn country.

The Fever Chart opens with *Vision One: A State of Innocence*,
set in something resembling a zoo but more silent, empty, in
Rafah, Palestine in 2002. The three characters in the play become
the caged animals, trapped in a barren and bleak world unable
to escape their past actions, memories and death. Yuval, the zoo
keeper, is unsure how he arrived at the zoo but is keen to maintain
the order of silence by killing any animal, child or adult that
makes a singing or gurgling sound. Shlomo, the architect, wants
to carry out his work, but is restricted by the soldiers who refuse
to let him pass the checkpoint. But an older, rebellious, fearless
Palestinian woman, Um Hisham, is haunted by a memory that

supersedes their daily grind. Um Hisham is mourning the death of her child Asma, who was killed by an Israeli bullet to the chest as she fed the pigeons on the roof. The grieving mother, distraught that her daughter died alone, has lost her faith in God and spends every day visiting the zoo. As the story about Asma unravels, so does her connection to Yuval; she informs him that he was also shot in her house by Israeli soldiers after he stopped them from beating her husband and then accepted a cup of tea, which resulted in the soldiers killing him, arresting her husband and bulldozing her house. Suddenly the place becomes a vision of purgatory, binding a Palestinian woman with a Tel Aviv Israeli man together by their experience of loss.

Vision Two: Between This Breath and You is set in a clinic waiting room in West Jerusalem, present day. Mourid, a Palestinian father, arrives at the private clinic two hours after closing time, demanding to see nurse Tanya Langer. The newly appointed mopper does his best to obstruct Mourid from seeing the nurse so that he can retire for the day, without any joy. The calm, straight-talking Tanya Langer enters the waiting room after working on her feet for ten hours and reluctantly agrees to give Mourid five minutes of her time. Unable to find anything medically wrong with Mourid, she soon becomes suspicious of his intentions and demands that he leave. But Mourid reveals personal information about Tanya's unqualified nursing status that puzzles her, as she is due to receive her qualifications in eighteen months' time. The events become more unsettling for Tanya when Mourid talks about his deceased son Ahmed and the real reason why he travelled from the West Bank to West Jerusalem to seek her out. Mourid believes that his Palestinian son is living through the young Israeli nurse literally and figuratively, due to a double lung transplant carried out five years ago after Tanya was diagnosed with cystic fibrosis. Tanya is quick to dismiss the allegations, but when Mourid talks profoundly about her disruptive sleeping patterns, recurring nightmares of suffocation and ways of coping with her erratic shortness of breath, she has no choice but to believe him.

Vision Three: The Retreating World is a monologue of heartbreaking stories from an Iraqi bird keeper named Ali from

Baghdad. A charming and witty Ali enters the space balancing a book on his head, before addressing the audience at the International Pigeon Convention. His speech about birds dates back to when he was just fifteen years old – the start of his hobby of collecting and trading birds. His obsession for birds is equally shared with his love for books, a passion which bonds him with his best friend Samar Saboura. As the play develops, we soon realize that the birds and books symbolize loss of freedom, death of loved ones and austerity caused by the Gulf War in Iraq. With no access to schools and limited medication, Ali's world suddenly shrinks and he is left to cope with unimaginable situations – such as his grandmother's need for little pink pills, which resulted in her dying in his arms. After the war, Ali is forced to sell his beloved books and twelve pigeons, as well as family heirlooms, for food and aspirins. As the trees die and the pigeons disappear, Ali says his final goodbye to his friend, Samir Saboura.

Summary (extract)

This speech has been extracted from the end of *Vision Three: The Retreating World*.

Ali (late twenties), casually but carefully dressed in slacks and a button-down shirt, talks at an International Pigeon Convention. **Ali** reveals the painful story of how he lost his pigeons and his closest and only friend, Samir Saboura.

Ali I don't know what love is. It goes. It comes. It goes. It comes. Samir Saboura. My friend. If love is in pieces, then he was a piece of love.

Tall, tall, he was. A handsome fellow with big dark eyes but, and I must say it, he walked like a pigeon. Now, pigeons are not really meant to walk. Their state of grace is to fly. But if they must walk, they walk like Samir walked. Like this:

(*He walks like Samir, bobbing is head in and out, taking sure but awkward steps.*)

It's possible his great grandfather was a flamingo. Samir. He was intelligent and hilarious, but he had one fault: he could hardly read. He was terribly dyslexic. So we would do the reading for him. Samir was always carrying a book, and whoever he came upon, he would say 'Read to me.' He'd memorize whole passages that he would recite at the most inopportune of moments. For instance, I had food poisoning when I was sixteen. All day I sat on the toilet, rocking and moaning. And, I must say it, stinking as well. But Samir would not leave my side. He would not leave me to suffer alone. Up and down the hallway outside the bathroom he strode, reciting pieces of Hart Crane. While I sputtered and farted in agony, snatches of *The Bridge* sailed in and out of my consciousness and kept me from despair:

(*He quotes Samir reciting Hart Crane.*)

'And if they take your sleep away sometimes They give it back again. Soft sleeves of sound attend the darkling harbour, the pillowed bay.'

A good friend, Samir. He had a library that even his teachers envied. He couldn't read the books himself, but he slept and ate among them. Running his big hands over their spines, he would grin at us: 'I cannot read them, but I can touch them.' He was so intimate with his books that he could close his eyes and find a book by its smell.

(*He tears a small piece of paper from a book and smells it, then eats it.*)

Books can also, in extreme times, be used as sustenance. But such eating makes for a parched throat. Many mornings I wake and I am thirsty. I turn on the taps but there is no running water. A once-modern city of three million people, with no running water for years now. The toilets are dry because we have no sanitation. Sewage pools in the streets. When we wish to relieve ourselves, we squat beside the dogs. At night, we turn on the lights to read the books we have forgotten we have sold, but there is no electricity. We go to the cupboard to eat cold cans of soup but there is no food processing so the cupboards are bare. A couple of us wanted to write a few polite words of complaint to the United Nations Sanctions Committee, but it has blocked the import of pencils as it is feared they might be used for making 'weapons of mass destruction'. Just recently it was reported that despite the blockade, at the very tops of some of the most remote mosques, nests have been found made entirely of pencils. (*Whispers*) Stockpiling.

(*He opens the book again.*)

Sometimes, if the occasion is right, a book is for reading.

(*He snaps the book shut. Then recites quietly.*)

Some say the world will end in fire, Some say ice. From what I've tasted of desire, I hold with those who favor fire.

Robert Frost. You teach that in school. 88,500 tons of bombs. Write this down without pencils: the equivalent of seven and a half atomic bombs of the size that incinerated Hiroshima. 900 tons of radioactive waste spread over much of what was once the land of dates. (*He gets rid of the book.*) Somewhere within this information is a lullaby.

(*Sings a piece of the Arab lullaby that he sung before. Beat.*)

And this, my friends, is documented. Fact. Fact. By the European Parliament, 1991. Members of the committee recorded the testimony, drinking cups of cold coffee: the defeated troops were surrendering. We, a nation of 'unpeople', were surrendering. Samir and myself, alongside seven hundred other men. We were dirty and tired and hungry, sucking orange mints because the napalm made our gums bleed. That morning, I'd relieved myself beside the others while invisible jets broke the black glass sky across the horizon. My friend Samir did the same.

And then we walked towards the American unit to surrender, our arms raised beside seven hundred other men.

(**Ali** *raises his arms.*)

Samir, he said to me – this is not documented – He said: 'I want to put my hands in a bucket of cold water.' Shut up, I said, keep your hands up. Samir said, 'I want to smell the back of my father's neck.' Shut up, I said. Shut up. We're almost home. Samir Saboura said, 'I want to tell an astonishing joke until you cry for relief.'

As we walked towards them – this is documented – the commander of the US unit fired, at one man, an anti-tank missile. A missile meant to pierce armour. At one man. The rest of us, arms still raised, stopped walking. I remember. I remember.

(**Ali** *slowly lowers his arms.*)

I could not. I could not recognize. My friend Samir. A piece of his spine stuck upright in the sand. His left hand blown so high in the air it was still falling. Then they opened fired on the rest of us.

A bullet hit me in the back as I ran. Out of hundreds, thousands in that week, a handful of us survived. I lived. Funny. That I am still here. The dead are dead. The living, we are the ghosts. We no longer say goodbye to one another. With the pencils we do not have we write our names so the future will know we were here. So that the past will know we are coming.

(*He quotes.*)

'In a world that seems so very puzzling is it any wonder birds have such appeal? Birds are, perhaps, the most eloquent expression of reality.'

Roger Tory Peterson, American Ornithologist, born 1908.

(*He quotes again.*)

'War is hell.'

Pete Williams, Defence department spokesman, on confirming that US army earth movers buried alive, in their trenches, up to 8,000 Iraqi soldiers. (*Beat.*) Yep. Yep. War is hell. And birds are perhaps the most eloquent expression of reality. In Arabic we say:

(*Says in Arabic, twice, the equivalent of 'fuck that'.*)

Which is the equivalent of: 'fuck that'.

I sold my last bird a few days ago. Tomorrow I will sell the cage. The day after that I will have nothing more to sell. But I keep track of the buyers, and who the buyers sell to. I go to their homes and I ask for the bones. Usually the family is kind, or frightened of me, and they give me the bones after the meal. I boil the bones and keep them in a bucket.

(*We now notice an old steel bucket that is elsewhere on stage. He takes the bucket.*)

Listen.

(*He shakes the bucket a few times. We hear the sound of bones rattling.*)

It is a kind of music.

(*He holds the bucket out to the audience.*)

These are the bones of those who have died, from the avenue of palms, from the land of dates. I have come here to give them to you for safekeeping. (*Beat.*) Catch them. If you can.

(*He throws the contents of the bucket at the audience. Instead of bones, into the air and across the audience spill hundreds of white feathers.*)

From

THE ADVENTURES OF ALI and ALI AND THE AXES OF EVIL

a divertimento for warlords

by Marcus Youssef, Guillermo Verdecchia and Camyar Chai

A co-production between NeWorlds Theatre (Vancouver) and Cahoots Theatre Projects (Toronto), *Ali and Ali* was performed at the Vancouver East Cultural Centre at Theatre Passe Muraille (Toronto) and at Montréal, Arts Interculturel in January 2004. The production was directed by Guillermo Verdecchia with the following cast: Marcus Youssef (Ali Ababwa), Camyar Chai (Ali Hakim/Dr Mohandes Panir/Ali Zia), Tom Butler (Tim/ Duncan/Osama) and Guillermo Verdecchia (Jean Paul Jacques Beauderrièredada). The play was later presented in Edmonton as part of the Magnetic North Festival at the Varscona Theatre with John Murphy in the roles of Tim, Duncan and Osama.

Ali and Ali is a fast, witty, unpredictable and hilariously funny play, which draws most of its material from War on Terror and related media headlines. The play adopts an unconventional approach to storytelling combining puppetry, political cabaret sketches and slapstick comedy to poke fun as well as punching jabs at politicians and their policies, together with the numerous emotive media reports, exposing the propaganda, contradictions, acts of distraction and hypocrisies deployed by those in power. Through these issues, the play comments on the audiences of today and their failure to dismantle, challenge or analyse the information that has been carefully constructed for them. At the heart of the play is a question about humanity, investigating our ability to connect, and show compassion for those who are suffering at the hands of the New World Order.

A refreshing break from conventional theatrical form, this play within several plays of powerful and thought-provoking sketches is centred on two protagonists: Ali Hakim and Ali Ababwa, who are from the fictional homeland Agraba. Ali and Ali are stateless refugees with UN identity papers used to performing their show in war zones. But today, they have successfully booked into a Canadian theatre by promising the theatre manager a multicultural, ethnic family drama. As the play develops, we realize that the actors have no intention of performing an 'ethnic family drama'; their sketches attacking the New World Order are abruptly interrupted by the theatre manager, who reinforces their agreement. Ali and Ali quickly improvise songs about togetherness and short scenes to appease him, but after a while revert back to their original content.

Throughout the production the characters in the play are aware of the audience and frequently improvise scenes or engage in conversation with them, trying to convince members of the audience to give them food, money, refuge, freedom and other material benefits of Western consumer society, falling miserably at every step.

Summary (extract)

Ali Hakim's bride has called. While **Ali Ababwa** is left alone on the stage, he decides to try his luck at securing a wife from the audience.

Ali Ababwa   Ali Hakim's bride. She is phoning from detention centre in Malta. She traded food for phone call. They were separated in the confusion and the pig of a smuggler took her money and instead of taking her and her family across the mountains to meet Ali Hakim, he drove her straight to Maltese detention centre where she is stranded without papers and expecting a baby in a few months. I am to be godfather. But how will she get out? Ali Hakim is wandering Agrabanian: stateless. He cannot send for her. Crazy life.

Tell Ana to take care of herself. She must eat for two. Not waste food on phone calls.

He turns back to audience.

Look at Ali Hakim, he is smiling. Oh my friend is a lucky man.

Ali Hakim *goes offstage to continue his call in private.* **Ali Ababwa** *tiptoes to centre stage.*

So, I'm single, pretty smart, sometimes amusing and somewhat exotic. I like long walks, dancing a bit strangely, and going to the theatre if I can leave at intermissions. When they have an intermission.

On the liability side, my bum is more or less constantly sore and though I have no children of my own (*sighs*), I do have dependents, many dependents, all of whom depend on me to send money home to buy food, water, and medicine.

He sings an excerpt from 'I Want to Be Loved by You'.

So – any takers? Ian, what do you say? Is OK, I am very open-minded. No, you are right. Two famous handsome brown men in one household – it would be all ego.

He picks a woman from the audience and approaches her.

How about you, madam? What do you say? Is easy, if immigration interrogates you, all you have to do is convince them of our intimacy. And believe me, once you've had Agrabanian you never go back. Please. I don't want to go back.

He retreats.

Oh, sure. Typical. You Canadians. You're so nuce and liberal and I support same-sex marriages and when you walk down the street and see a woman with a dot on her forehead, you think that's pretty cool and maybe you even have dot envy. But when it comes to blue Agrabanians, well that's a whole different story now, isn't it? Oh, yes you believe blue Agrabanians should share the same rights and privileges as you and no you would never discriminate against blue Agrabanians and yes you think hate-crimes legislation should be rewritten to include blue Agrabanians but do you think blue is sexxxxxyyyy?

He returns to the woman.

Kiss me and I'll shut up. Is true. Just one. On the cheek. Blue is permanent – won't come off on lips, I promise.

Ad-libbing as necessary until she – or he – does.

(*after kiss*) Be still my beating heart.

(**Voice over***: According to Agrabanian Traditional Law, if a woman kisses a man they are deemed to have been married since they were 13 – and all property reverts to the male.*)

May I have keys to late model luxury sedan? Credit card? You will find that I can adapt quickly to your carefree lifestyle. Please, I beg you, take me with you.

From

I CALL MY BROTHERS

by Jonas Hassen Khemiri

translated by Rachel Willson-Broyles

I Call My Brothers toured Sweden with Riksteatern in 2013, directed by Farnaz Arbabi, and premiered in New York in January 2014. The Australian premiere was presented by Melbourne Theatre Company at Southbank Theatre, The Lawler on 16 April 2015, directed by Nadja Kostich with the following cast: Osamah Sami (Amor), Ray Chong Nee (Shvi/Amplifier/ Bully/The Salesman), Joana Pires (Amplifier/Bully/Valeria/ Karolina), Alice Ansara (Amplifier/Ahlem/The Supervisor/ Tyra). It has also been performed in Norway, Denmark, Germany (multiple theatres), France, Spain, Finland and London (at the Arcola Theatre). Most recently, *I Call My Brothers* returned to the Arcola Theatre as part of Volta International Festival on 3 September 2015, directed by Yael Shavit with the following cast: Amber Aga, Nabil Elouahabi, Rachid Sabitri and Siubhan Harrison.

Swedish playwright Jonas Hassen Khemiri's play *I Call my Brothers* is a humorous and yet deeply disturbing response to an actual event which took place in central Stockholm in 2010. The play began as an essay published in *Dagens Nyheter* in December 2010, one week after a suicide bombing in central Stockholm that dramatically changed the nation. An Iraqi-born Swedish citizen was identified as the perpetrator of a failed suicide attack as well as a second nearby bomb which exploded shortly afterwards, resulting only in his death. Although the incident did not cause a mass killing, it did have a catastrophic impact on the Islamic community and a country that was once considered one of the most liberal nations in the world. After the event, which was branded a terrorist attack by the media, the Swedish community became fearful, suspicious and paranoid of the Muslim community, causing an increase in police presence and the introduction of an operation called REVA – legalizing police profiling whereby the police could stop, search and deport illegal immigrants. Under REVA, many Muslims were targeted, subjected to violent harassment by the police and asked to provide proof of identity to confirm that they were part of the nation.

Kherimi sets his play just a few moments before the suicide bombing in Stockholm to give an account from the perspective of the Muslim community whose lives were never the same after the attack. The story is told through the eyes of a Muslim lead character, Amor, who narrates a non-chronological abstract story of his life with flashbacks from his carefree school days, where his only problem was selecting the right periodical element to match his school friends' personas, to fearing walking the streets of his hometown. With the support of an ensemble cast who play different characters (including his deceased grandmother), we enter Amor's head to experience his subconscious mind, imagined thoughts and physical barriers. In a world incited by attitudes of fear, paranoia and prejudice, the lines between reality and fiction, innocence and guilt become even more blurred.

Amor's journey begins on what seems to be an ordinary Saturday night of drinking and dancing at a nightclub while avoiding his demanding best friend Shavi's phone calls. But we quickly realize that this is no ordinary night. Amor's mood suddenly changes when he decides to retrieve Shavi's voicemail messages and learns about the bombings. The nightmare begins as the bomber's identity is revealed as an Iraqi-born Muslim male. Now targeted as a prospective terrorist, Amor tries to adopt a non-threatening 'normal' demeanour, but how does one successfully walk, talk and act to diminish the fears and prejudice attitudes of others, without beginning to doubt yourself?

I Call my Brothers is a powerful and harrowing story about Islamophobia, racial profiling, paranoia and guilt.

Summary (extract)

Amor is on his way home. He is still in the city centre. He has begun to confuse fiction with reality, questioning his involvement in the attack. He narrates the story as it plays in his mind.

Amor   Then it was night and I would be home soon, I walked
toward the subway, I saw a person standing and swaying in front
of a display window, he was holding a packet of French fries
in his hand like it was a baby bird, he slurred something, I kept
walking, I was on my way home, I wasn't far from the bus stop
when I saw the police car. The sirens were off so they wouldn't
attract attention but you could tell that something was going on
because the one cop turned his head toward his shoulder and
called for backup and the other cop slowly placed his hand on
the holster and the guy they had caught was pressed up against
the bridge railing and the one cop had one hand on his holster
and the guy looked afraid, he met my eyes, I saw the color of his
hair, I thought 'enough is enough' and I came closer, my steps
were lead, my eyes were neon, my arms were arsenic, the police
officers stood with their backs to me and they were crowding the
guy and he was my brother, he needed my help, they were going
to arrest him, they were going to deport him, they were going to
shoot him, they had forced him out of the car, the hazard lights
were blinking, the police car was dark, his car was lit up, they
had seen his license plate, they had suspected drugs or smuggling
or bodies, they had already called for backup, and soon the
dogs will be here, and the bulletproof vests and the visors and
the horses and the helicopters and the batons and the tear gas
and as I got closer I remembered the policeman who jumped on
Houda's cousin and beat him bloody with the butt of his baton
just because he talked back and the Securitas guards who broke
Nasim's shin and then accused him of assault on an officer and
Maribel's sister who wasn't allowed into that soul club and when
she started yelling discrimination security called the police and
the police came and found a bag of weed in her purse even though
she'd never smoked weed in her life and she said herself that she
didn't even understand that it was grass when the police took it
out because she thought grass looked more like grass and less like
moss and so she tried to get off by saying: 'that's not grass, that's
moss', and the police looked at her like she was completely nuts
and much later, after she'd received the letter with her sentence,
after she'd paid the fines, after she'd been nervous that her next
employer would look up her criminal record, she said that the

worst part was the looks they gave her when she tried to explain
that it wasn't hers and she had been set up, that it was all a lie,
because they looked at her with smiles that said: 'Yes, we know
that's what's going on, but what are you going to do about it, what
are you going to do?' And I remembered the plainclothes cops and
Ahlem and the lifeguard and Monkey Mountain and I approached
the police, they had the guy surrounded, he didn't know Swedish,
he was gesticulating wildly, he feared for his life, a car door was
open and his family was sitting in there and I saw the contours of
the mom and the children, the streetlights and the reflections and
the stars in the sky and the mom was on her way out, one foot on
the asphalt, she wanted to help, she wanted to explain, she wanted
to protect but she didn't need to because I was already there, I
was light as lithium, I was self-igniting like phosphorus, I had my
hand on my pocket, I snuck the knife out, I felt its weight and hid
the blade against my forearm. The first policeman didn't have a
chance, I stabbed him in the back and I, policeman number two
reached for his weapon but didn't get more than halfway before
the knife punctured his stomach and the blood flowed and the
bridge swayed and police dogs were coming and I killed them too
and a patrol on horseback came and I split them right in half and a
helicopter came and I threw the knife straight into the propeller so
that it first slowly and then quickly crashed down into the black-
as-night sea where everything was mirror images and upside-down
buildings and just before I came up to them I heard the first
policeman say: (*Swinglish*) 'No, no, it's not difficult at all,' and
the other policeman said: 'Just listen to him now,' and the first
one said: 'You go straight, you hear me you go straight over this
bridge and then the first one to the right and you take that street
and you follow it okay? You follow it and you go and go and go
and then when you reach the roundabout there's the sign to the
highway' and the guy said 'Right then straight, okay', 'You got it
now?' 'I hope so thank you' and the dad went back to the car and
the light went off when he closed the door and the police looked at
each other and smiled and shook their heads and then they caught
sight of a strange guy who was standing there crying farther away
on the bridge, they approached him, they said: 'Hey, you, are you
okay' and the guy just refused to answer, he refused to answer, he

was crying even though he didn't have a reason and there was a splash from down by the water, he had thrown something into the water, it glittered on the bottom, maybe it was a knife or maybe it was a worn out drill head and when the police came up to him he turned around and ran in the opposite direction and the police just wanted to ask a few questions so they started running after him, a little slowly at first but the guy ran faster and the police sped up and called for backup, 'we have a person on a bridge his description is' so and so and the police radio screamed out his appearance and police ears listened and police hands turned wheels in the direction of the guy who obviously had something to hide but he who was him who was mehad already run one bridge and four blocks then turned left after a park and then up some stairs and then down into a parking lot and then into a 24-hour 7-11 and out through the other entrance and soon he had been swallowed up by the city he had disappeared he snuck around like a hidden shadow among shadows and he was asphalt and bike lanes and curbs and he was beyond saving and he hardly noticed when his phone rang but soon he noticed it and dried two kinds of salty taste off his face and he answered he said: Hello and he imagined that his voice sounded normal. Hello, he said. Hello. Is anyone there?

Thirties

From

THE MOUNTAINTOP

by Katori Hall

The Mountaintop was developed during the Lark Play
Development Center Barebones workshop in New York in April
2009 and received its world premiere at Theatre503, London
in June 2009, followed by a transfer a month later to Trafalgar
Studios, London. The London production was directed by James
Dacre, with the following cast: Lorraine Burroughs (Camae) and
David Harewood (Dr Martin Luther King, Jr). *The Mountaintop*
won an Olivier Award for Best New Play in 2010, and opened in
Broadway's Bernard B. Jacobs Theatre, New York City in October
2011, directed by Kenny Leon, starring Angela Bassett (Camae)
and Samuel L. Jackson (Dr Martin Luther King, Jr).

Katori Hall's play *The Mountaintop* is gripping, imaginative and
hilarious. The play excellently captures the man behind the 'Dr
Martin Luther King' title to reveal him as a human being with
fears, disappointments, insecurities and ego. Hall accomplishes her
intention to humanize Dr Martin Luther King in order to enable
us to appreciate how an ordinary man became one of the world's
greatest revolutionary civil rights leaders, in the hope that we will
be inspired to recognize our own capabilities, strength and power.

The Mountaintop is set in the infamous Lorraine Motel in Room
306, the night before Dr Martin Luther King's assassination.
Earlier that day King delivered a famous speech at the Memphis
church to a congregation of a couple of thousand people. As he
waits in the hotel room for close associate Rev. Ralph Abernathy
to return with his Pall Mall cigarettes, he rehearses the words of a
future speech 'Why America is going to hell', relieving himself in
the motel toilet. But when King returns to the bedroom and calls
for room service to request a cup of coffee, Katori's drama turns
into magical realism.

An unknown, mysteriously attractive young maid named Camae
arrives with coffee for King only a few moments after he has
put down the receiver. As luck would have it, Camae smokes

the same cigarettes as King, which she pulls out almost from
nowhere. Camae's sassy and straight-talking nature, together with
a shared love for Pall Malls, swiftly puts King at ease. Captivated
by her beauty and amused by her opposing views on political
action, which are more in line with his rival, Malcolm X, the two
effortlessly exchange banter and pedestrian conversation.

The atmosphere abruptly changes when Camae accidently refers
to King by his birth name, Michael. King's paranoia surfaces
and he immediately becomes suspicious of Camae's true identity
and intentions. He suspects that she is a spy who intends to tear
his family apart by recording their conversation and sending it to
his wife, to suggest an act of infidelity. Fearful that he is being
set up for the second time, he attempts to throw her out of his
motel room. Camae is forced to confess that she is an angel sent
to inform and prepare him for his impending death, while King is
forced to come to terms with his mortality, failures and regrets.

This is a play about dreams, hopes and letting go.

Summary (extract)

King (Dr Martin Luther King, Jr), a thirty-nine-year-old Nobel
Peace Prize-winning civil rights movement leader, has been
informed by the angel **Camae** of his impending assassination.
In his desperation to stay alive for the forthcoming march on the
Washington Mall, a campaign that he has worked on tirelessly
over the last year, he snatches the cordless phone to speak to **God**.

King   God, Ma'am. You don't sound like I thought You'd sound.
No, no, no. Pardon me, if that offends. I like how You sound.
Kinda like my grandmama. Well … it is a compliment. I loved
her dearly … I love You more, though. Camae told me that you
might be busy tonight. Oh, You have time for me? For one of Your
favorites?

He smiles at **Camae**, *who rolls her eyes.*

God, are You all right? You sound hoarse. Oh, You tired? Well it
must be tiring to be everywhere all at the same time (*He laughs
nervously.*) Well, God … I don't mean to trouble You, Ma'am, but
I wanted to ask You something … You see I have always listened
to You, honored Your word, lived by Your word – (*He lowers his
voice.*) for the most part – (*Raises it back to normal.*) God, please
don't strike me down for askin' this, but … I want to live. I have
plans. Lots of plans in my head and in my heart and my people need
me. They need me. And I need to see them to the Promised Land.
(*Beat.*) I know that's not what I said earlier tonight, I know, but
… I wasn't lying exactly. (*He looks at* **Camae**.) I just didn't know
she was comin' so, so … soon. I meant every word I said tonight
when I spoke to those people. Dead honest! No pun intended …
God, I just … I wanna see my people there, the tide is turning …
war is becoming the order of the day and I must, I must convince
them to be vigilant … We've come too far to turn back now …
God, listen to me … Who else is betta fit for this job? I mean, who
will take my place? (*He hears Her answer.*) JESSE?! (*Pause.*)
I – I – I just thought Ralph would make a better – No, no, no, no,
I have not turned vain. On the contrary. I'm but a servant for You,
God, Ma'am. Yes, I've been a servant for You all my life. At one
point in time, I might nota been up for the challenge but I knew
this was all par for the course and I did Your will. I honored YOUR
WILL, God, Ma'am. Let me not die a man who doesn't get to hug
his children one last time. Let me not die a man who never gets to
make love to his wife one last time. Let me not be a man who dies
afraid and alone. (*Long pause.*) Then why'd You pick me, huh?
Hmm, no disrespect, but if You didn't know what I could do, what
my (*hissing*) *talents* were then … You got some nerve. Dragging
me here to this moldy motel room in Memphis. To die. HUH! Of

all places! Well, I *am* angry. There have been many a' nights when I have held my tongue when it came to You. But not tonight, NOT TONIGHT. I have continuously put my life on the line, gave it all up. Gave it all up for You and Your word. You told me, that I'd be safe. Safe in Your arms. You protected me all this time, all this time! Glued a pair of wings to my back, but now that've I've flown too close to the sun I'm falling into the ocean of death. God how dare You take me now? NOW! I beg of You. I plead – God? Ma'am? God?

Long heavy silence.

I think … I think she hung up on me.

From

GOOD GOODS

by Christina Anderson

Good Goods received its world premiere at Yale Repertory
Theatre on 3 February 2012, directed by Tina Landau with the
following cast: Marc Damon Johnson (Truth), Oberon K.A.
Adjepong (Waymon as Hunter Priestess, Factory folk), de'Adre
Aziza (Patricia), Kyle Beltran (Wire), Clifton Duncan (Stacey) and
Angela Lewis (Sunny).

African American playwright Christina Anderson merges drama
with spirituality to create a riveting play which explores the many
facets of love, identity and possession. Set in a fictitious small
black town in 'the South' (of America) – a place you have to
know about to get to it and know someone from there to survive –
Anderson draws on key historical references over several decades
between 1961 and 1994 to unleash the town's mysterious history.
In the world of *Good Goods* everything is transient, including
relationships, staff, and even the ownership of bodies. One thing
that remains constant is the convenience store, 'Good Goods',
where all the action in the play takes place. When the owner,
Mr Good Senior, suffers an incident and runs away, the store's
long-standing and only employee, Truth, expects to become the
sole proprietor. But before he can get his feet under the desk, Mr
Good Senior's son, Stacey Good, arrives at the store ready to
take over. Tension mounts between Truth and Stacey – although
Truth has years of experience as well as a verbal promise from
Mr Good, he cannot fight the written declaration noted on the
paperwork which gives Stacey legal rights to the store, but is
desperate not to work at the factory.

But that's not the only complication in Stacey's life. He was
previously part of a comedy duo with a woman called Patricia
(known as Patty), abandoning both abruptly to carry out his family
duty in the shop. Patricia arrives to confront Stacey; it's also the
birthday of her twin brother Wire, which she claims is the sole
reason why she has returned home. She is joined by a runaway

bride, Sunny, whom she met on the bus, who instantly becomes Truth's love interest. The relationship between Patricia and Stacey is revealed to exceed more than a cabaret act. However, in the return to their childhood homes, romantic feelings from the past resurface, and the reunion between Wire and Stacey reignites an old flame, which leads to a heated argument exposing the truth about their secret homosexual love affair. Amongst the unleashing of hidden secrets, the spirit that Sunny is channelling called Hunter Priestess enters the room, possessing Sunny's body with the spirit of a young boy, Emekah, who recently died in a fatal accident at the factory.

Summary (extract)

Truth is a thirty-five-year-old black American man, the shop assistant and watch guard of Good Goods. After working at the store since he was a boy, he has become bitter with age and broken promises. **Mr Good Senior** promised that if he had a daughter, Truth could marry her and take over his business. However, as luck would have it, the daughter turned out to be a son, Stacey Good, inevitably robbing him of both dreams. But now he has met Sunny, he believes his luck has changed.

Truth and **Stacey** stand inside the shop. After **Stacey** implies that **Truth** knows less than him because he hasn't travelled outside of their hometown, **Truth** hits back by revealing the truth about his father's health, self-sacrifices and his shattered dreams for the future.

Author's Note

Given the context of the scene, the =.= indicates an active moment of gesture or a moment of communication that transcends language.

Truth   Do you know why your daddy had to jet outta town?

[…]

=.=

Huh?

[…]

He got chased out.

=.=

=.=

And not by no debt or no affair …

Not by what you can see, but what you can feel.

=.=

=.=

=.=

Said the Devil was after him. Trying to possess his soul.

Said he'd be in bed in that back room just like you do now and he'd open his eyes to the Devil standin over him, pissin fire on his sheets.

=.=

=.=

He stopped sleepin.

=.=

Made me sit up with him thru the night with a rifle in my lap and a .45 in his.

Me. I did that for your daddy.

=.=

He kept getting worse and worse. I couldn't keep a hold of him.

=.=

=.=

You a waste, Stacey. Ain't worth the pot you shit in …

[…]

=.=

[…]

Disappointment.

[…]

You think you funny?

You ain't. Patty makes me laugh. But you, you make me cry. Make a grown man cry –

[…]

Cause all this was supposed to be mine!

=.=

=.=

All of this was promised to me and I can't leave it.

I won't leave it. You were supposed to be a girl! You were promised to me! I was supposed to be your husband! You was supposed to come out a girl and I was gonna marry you and your daddy was gonna give me this damn shop!

When I was six years old he promised me … promised me … right at that counter. Said I was gonna marry his daughter. Be his son. He said I could add on a house in the back to raise a family in …

=.=

I was crying the whole way when I ran to tell your daddy how you came out. I thought he was gonna be upset. I thought he was gonna be disappointed that he couldn't have me … but, but he was happy.

That muthafucka was overjoyed!

=.=

And just like that … I ain't got nothin. Or nobody. All I do is watch this fuckin shop day in, day out. Sweep the damn floors, clean the windows. But none of it is mine. Never will be … I felt like I ain't had no plan B for most of my life.

'Til today. 'Til that gal walked thru that door with that smile …

From

DETROIT '67

by Dominique Morisseau

Detroit '67 was developed at the Lark Play Development Center, New York. The play was further developed and originally produced in New York by the Public Theater in association with the Classical Theatre Harlem and the National Black Theatre, on 12 March 2013. This production was directed by Kwame Kwei-Armah with the following cast: Francois Battiste (Lank), Michelle Wilson (Chelle), De'Adre Aziza (Bunny), Brandon J. Dirden (Sly) and Samantha Soule (Caroline).

Dominique Morisseau was awarded a 2014 Edward M. Kennedy Prize for Drama Inspired by American History for her play *Detroit '67*, the first part of a trilogy based on the writer's hometown of Detroit. As the title implies, the play is set in Detroit during 1967, notorious for one of the most deadly riots in US history, as well as the celebrated success of Motown music. Morisseau seamlessly combines the bitter devastation of the riots against the sweet soothing music of legendary artists such as the Temptations, Marvin Gaye and the Vandellas to create a haunting tale about the complexities of life as a black person in Detroit during this era. Morisseau effortlessly captures a time of segregation, oppression, economic deprivation and racial tension but also offers a sense of hope through the ambition of co-protagonist Lank, an aspiring business owner who refuses to let his heart be hardened by racism.

Siblings Michelle (known as Chelle) and Langston (named after Langston Hughes and referred to as Lank) are left orphaned after the recent loss of their father. With a substantial inheritance, the two have opposing ideas of how best to spend the money. Practical single parent Chelle is determined to use the money sensibly by paying off the house and her son's tuition fees, continuing to make ends meet through their illegal after-hours basement parties. But Chelle's young brother, Lank, a loving, charismatic dreamer, has his heart set on buying the Sheplings Bar with his best friend-cum-business partner Sylvester (simply known as Sly) and thus becoming the first black legitimate business owner. Not easily impressed, Chelle is not sold on his pipe dream.

Things become even more complicated when Lank and Sly bring home a white girl, Caroline, whom they discovered abandoned and battered on the street. Chelle is horrified to discover a white girl in their home and orders the guys to get rid of her. Lank and Sly are fearful that people may wrongfully accuse them of being the perpetrators of her assault and worry about the repercussions if they take her to the hospital or return her to the sidewalk. With that in mind they plea for Chelle to let her stay for the night. Chelle grudgingly agrees.

With nowhere to go and no money, Caroline becomes a lodger, earning her stay by helping the family with their after-hours basement parties. We soon discover Caroline's colourful past, now on the run from her violent racist cop boyfriend, who habitually targeted and physically abused innocent black men. The night Lank and Sly found her she had become the target of his abuse and tried to escape. Chelle does not trust Caroline, but Lank and Caroline have fallen in love with each other.

Meanwhile, Lank and Sly secretly buy the Sheplings Bar. But when police raid Dukes' after-hours joint located near the Sheplings Bar and badly beat up Buddy Johnson and Martha Briggs, the black community get mad and retaliate by fighting the police and burning the city. As Detroit goes up in flames, Lank tries to save his building, dreams and inheritance.

Summary (extract)

Lank (early thirties, cool, loving and charismatic) has returned from the rioted streets of Detroit and the Sheplings Bar. He comes back to the house with the signed deeds in his hand but without his best friend and business partner **Sly**, who has been killed by the police. To make things worse the love of his life, **Caroline**, has fled from the state before he returns home, thanks to his sister **Chelle**, who detested the idea of her brother dating a white girl.

Lank   I know Chelle. (*Beat.*) I know you … you see her and you
see me and you ain't like it. I know. And I … I don't know what
to say 'bout it. I just know she wasn't half bad. When I talked to
her sometimes I just felt … like myself. Like I remembered what
I can do. Like all the rules put on me cuz of this or that or where
I'm from or what I am … it was possible to break 'em all and still
have somethin' … (*Pause.*) But I that wasn't real. The rules is the
rules, and soon as you step outside the space you been given, it
don't do nothin' you think it's gonna do. You thinkin' it's gonna
open the world up. All it do is upset the world and set it on fire.
All it do is make you lose your best buddy

I lost him, Chelle.

(*Beat.*)

I was there with him, til' the end. There when we signed the
papers in our name. There when he went runnin' after them
pigs who showed up tryin' to burn us down. Tryin' to send us a
message for bein' uppity. There when we chased after 'em. There
when them big tanks rolled 'round the corner. He ain't seein' what
I see. Told him stop. Don't run after. He ain't seen 'em rollin' up.
Them soldiers that come to back up the police for the riots. Saw
niggers chasin' after cops and decided the niggers were the ones to
shoot. And I was there when they shot him, Chelle. There when he
fell. Went back to him and lifted him in my arms. Felt his blood
soak my shirt. Saw his chest open –

I was there, Chelle. Til' the end. (*Beat.*) He was my best buddy.

And he's gone.

From

BOMBAY BLACK

by Anosh Irani

Bombay Black was commissioned and developed by
Nightswimming Theatre. Produced by Cahoots Theatre Project,
the play premiered at the Theatre Centre in Toronto, on 4 January
2006, directed by Brian Quirt with the following cast: Sanjay
Talwar (Kamal), Deena Aziz (Padma) and Anita Majumdar
(Apsara).

Indian-Canadian writer Anosh Irani won four Dora Awards for
Bombay Black, including Outstanding New Play. Irani adopts
Bombay's original name for the title and setting of his play
(instead of the city's new name, Mumbai), a device which
complements the story's combining of traditional Indian practices
in modern-day society to explore taboo subjects including child
marriages, paedophilia, betrayal and revenge. *Bombay Black* is
an unconventional love story between a blind man and a young
Indian dancer.

The setting is modern-day India, in an apartment overlooking the
Arabian Sea. Twenty-year-old dancer Aspara captures the interest of
wealthy punters through her beauty and sensual dances. Aspara is
managed by her mother Padma, who charges the men extortionate
amounts of money for the pleasure of watching her daughter dance
erotically, as well as selling illegal drugs: cocaine and Bombay
Black is a poisonous drug made by mixing hashish and shoe polish.
But beneath their seedy business dealings lies a hidden secret,
resulting in a petrified Aspara and a dangerously vengeful mother.

Since the age of five, Aspara has been tormented by a recurring
nightmare of smoke being in her eyes, a dream which she
struggles to make any sense of – a truth known by her mother,
who refuses to explain. She is also haunted by her father's
scent and voice. We soon discover that Aspara's biggest fear is
her father, who raped her when she was seven years old, and
continued to have an unconsented affair with his daughter with his
wife's knowledge. Mother and daughter absconded ten years ago,

and have not seen or heard from Aspara's father since. Instead Padma's resentment towards her husband and jealousy of her daughter's beauty and youthfulness has festered even more over the years. She tries to brainwash Aspara into thinking that all men are bad and not to be trusted. But when a mysterious blind man appears for his appointment with Aspara, the truth is revealed, secrets are exposed, and Aspara falls in love for the first time.

Bombay Black is a story about a girl who has to escape the physical and psychological grasp of mother and father to experience true love, independence and freedom.

Summary (extract)

Kamal, a blind man in his thirties, enlightens **Aspara** about the true story behind her recurring nightmares, how she took away his sight, and reveals that they are husband and wife – married by her father (a priest) when they were infants.

Kamal A dream? So you've converted our life into a dream.
That's okay with me. The crackling of wood can be heard even in
dreams. It starts slowly at first … faint … as though it isn't really
there …

You're three years old and you're dressed in yellow. Same colour
as the fire almost. You're circling around the fire and its smoke
is making your eyes water. But there are also tears. The sound
of the priest chanting. You're scared and so am I. Oh yes, I'm
right there with you. I'm ten years old. I'm scared too, and as
we circle the fire I look at you, a sorry three-year-old-girl, crying
for her mother, begging her to take you away. And I'm ashamed
of myself. Even though it's not my fault. I feel responsible for
making you scared. And all those people. Those stupid people,
stupid villagers with grins on their faces as though we were in a
circus, you and I, two little monkeys getting married. That's what
it felt like. We were monkeys forced to walk round a fire by our
parents. And then I did it. I touched you. I held your hand out of
pity because you were more scared than I. And the moment I did,
a blind flashing of light, like a rod of lightning had pierced my
eyes, as though my pupils had committed some horrible crime and
needed to be punished. And then it was I who was screaming for
my mother. I should have run into the flames, Aspara. I'm sorry
that I ran the other way, into the crowd. Into that dumb, sweaty,
brain-fucked crowd. (*Pause.*) So let me ask you now? Do you
know who I am?

She is nervous. She gets up. He senses this.

Don't try to leave.

He moves towards her.

You took my sight. Now, I want it back.

From

BELLS

by Yasmin Whittaker Khan

Produced by Kali Theatre Company, *Bells* by Yasmin Whittaker
Khan was first performed at Birmingham Repertory Theatre on 23
March 2005. This production was directed by Poonam Brah, with
the following cast: Damian Asher (Charles), Marc Elliott (Pepsi),
Shivani Ghai (Aiesha), Nicholas Khan (Ashraf) and Sharona
Sassoon (Madam).

British-Pakistani playwright Yasmin Whittaker Khan's powerful
drama exposes the underground world of a South Asian Mujra
nightclub in East London. Mujra (a traditional form of Indian
dance) nightclubs derived from Pakistan and date back many
centuries. The modern version of Mujra clubs have transformed
into forbidden seedy venues where scantily dressed Asian women
perform songs and erotically charged dances to Bollywood music
for money. In this world the lines between entertainment and
prostitution are blurred. There is a growing number and demand
for Mujra nightspots in London, involving girls and young men
from London, Indian and Pakistan who are expected to perform
in clubs and private functions for men (many of them devout
Muslims who are quick to condemn the practice in public), for
very little money. Inspired by research trips to some of the Mujra
clubs in London, Whittaker takes us on a hidden journey beneath
the bells, make-up and colourful shalwar kameez to portray
the loneliness, vulnerability, exploitation and psychological
intimidation that affects both the performers and the punters.

The play is set in a fictional Mujra called Bells which runs as
butchers by day and transforms into a Bollywood-style glitzy club
at night, jointly managed by Ashraf and Madam. The relationship
between the owners is tenuous, rapidly veering from yearning to
hatred. Moreover, Ashraf pretty much has his hands full chopping
raw meat, keeping Madam in line and exploiting his position as
the boss of the brothel by indulging in sexual encounters with
Pepsi, the transvestite courtesan. But at the heart of this story is

a young beautiful heroine named Aiesha, from the Kanjar caste, a community that is historically associated with prostitution. But Aiesha's story is even more unimaginable: at age thirteen she was raped and kidnapped by her father's enemies over land in Pakistan, then dropped off at Madam's in the middle of the night with nothing but the dirty bloody shawl she was wearing. Aiesha knows that she can never return to her beloved family and country, but she is determined to find a way out of the seedy Bells nightclub in East London, where extra cash guarantees sexual favours. But being Madam's favourite courtesan and popular with the male clients, her chances look very slim.

The members-only club usually runs like clockwork, but when they receive a visit from Charles, a British South Asian middle-class accountant, Madam's and Ashraf's nightmares become a reality. Charles falls deeply in love with Aiesha, offering her the chance of a new life away from prostitution, pain and degradation. Aiesha is ready to take the plunge – but will the owners be willing to let her go?

Bells highlights the hypocrisy, secrets and cycle of exploitation that exist to maintain the success of Mujras the world over.

Summary (extract)

Thirty-five-year-old **Charles** is a middle-class British Indian accountant working in London, but born and raised in Cambridgeshire. After several attempts at trying to win **Aiesha**'s attention by throwing money at her, paying for intimacy, buying her books and sending her Oscar Wilde's poetry, **Charles** has been reassured by **Pepsi** of **Aiesha**'s mutual love for him. He arrives at the Mujra to seal the deal. But in his absence, **Aiesha** has been sexually assaulted by the homosexual owner, **Ashraf**, leaving her not knowing who to trust.

Charles wears smart but casual-looking business suits, silk ties, and has a smart leather rucksack with him at all times. He wears a gold watch and a gold ring on his little finger.

Charles   (**Charles** *starts to kiss* **Aiesha** *from her feet to her shoulders. Aiesha carries on reading her book. Softly trying to get her attention and seduce her away from her book.*)

Aiesha. Come away with me. Be mine and only mine … you're beautiful, you're perfection, you're mine.

(*He holds on to her and hugs her.*)

Are you mine? Or am I just feeling this way alone … don't you feel for me what I feel for you. Could I not be Majnu and you be my Laila? You see I remembered … you're Laila Majnu and I'll build you a garden just like Tom's Midnight Garden.

Pause.

Aiesha speak to me. Come on put your book down … this is important. I've come to ask Ashraf and madam whether I can marry you. Well I should really get on my knees. Sorry about that.

But only if you feel the same. I don't want to force you into anything.

Pause.

I know we don't know much about each other but … it'll be fine.

We've got loads of time to do things together. We've got the rest of our lives.

I want to know about every book you read, about what makes you smile and what makes you sad. I want to know how to be perfect for you. You've filled what has been missing in me all my life, you're my culture, my Urdu, my poetry, my history and you're my future.

(*Kisses her on the lips*)

Talk to me my love … do you love me?

From

MUSTAFA

by Naylah Ahmed

A co-production between Kali Theatre Company and Birmingham Repertory Theatre, *Mustafa* was first performed at Birmingham Repertory Theatre on 7 March 2012, subsequently followed by a tour to London, Plymouth, Bradford, Birmingham and Manchester. The production was directed by the Artistic Director of Kali Theatre Company, Janet Steel, with the following cast: Munir Khairdin (Mustafa), Ryan Early (Dan), Paul McCleary (Len) and Gary Pillai (Shabir). *Mustafa* was nominated for four 'Offies' (Off West End Theatre Awards) and awarded second prize at the Royal National Theatre Foundation Award.

Birmingham writer Naylah Ahmed took inspiration to write a supernatural thriller from childhood horror stories of the evil djinn told by her Pakistani family. However, these same horror stories of people being possessed by djinn are expressed as real accounts known to happen in Pakistan and London, with numerous reports of exorcisms to extract these harmful creatures from human bodies and minds. *Mustafa* masterfully investigates the truth behind these stories, as well as exploring themes of power, violence, guilt and madness, to create a tale that challenges the way we think about supernatural existence.

The play is set in an isolated single occupancy cell in a previously abandoned wing of a UK prison, now allocated to the psychologically tormented lead character Mustafa, who has been sentenced to fourteen years for the manslaughter of a teenage boy during an exorcism. A young prison guard, Dan, searches the barely furnished cell looking for something to confiscate as repercussion for a fight that occurred in the prison dining room involving the troubled inmate Mustafa. But with the only personal belongings being a prayer mat, stick of chalk (which has been used to draw a circle on the floor in the centre of the cell), notebook and the Qur'an, his choices are limited.

Dan has grown immensely fearful of Mustafa, especially after witnessing the fight in the lunchtime dining room, when taunts from prisoner Tony sparked a mysterious and unexplainable sighting, causing him injuries. Despite Dan's trepidation, senior prison guard Len is not fazed by the assigned role of Mustafa's personal officer and is keen to confront him about the altercation and prevent any further incidents happening at the prison. Mustafa is still consumed with guilt from the loss of the teenage boy, losing the ability to eat or sleep; he wants nothing more than to carry out his sentence in isolation, away from the other prisoners. But Len has other ideas. Len is convinced that isolation will only incite further animosity and fear, and lead to many more altercations with prisoners. As Len articulates his masterplan, Mustafa grows intensely anxious, discovering his prayer mat, notebook and chalk have been taken from his cell. As the prison officer delivers his final comments to Mustafa, the lights begin to change subtly and Len's behaviour starts to change dramatically. Mustafa starts to believe that the evil djinn that he tried to abstract from the young boy's body has found a new body to rest in – his.

But is Mustafa a mere criminal or a selfless man who has jeopardized his life to save a young, innocent teenage boy? What is the truth behind this djinn horror story?

Summary (extract)

British Pakistani **Mustafa** is in his late thirties. In an attempt to reclaim his confiscated possessions he unenthusiastically leaves the confines of his prison cell to visit the recreation room. Observed by his personal prison officer **Len**, **Mustafa** makes no effort to join the other prisoners, taking to playing pool alone, using his own rules. **Len** rewards his efforts by placing his prayer mat and notebook on the table. But with **Mustafa** refusing to eat in the prison dining room, the guards are certain that he has a secret stash of food. **Mustafa** informs them that he is living off water and prayer and explains why being close to God by fasting at a time like this is vital for him to stay focused.

Due to the fact that he came to England as a child, **Mustafa** does not have an Asian accent; he is correct in his pronunciation of English, Arabic and Urdu words. He wears a thaveez on a black cord around his neck throughout the play.

Mustafa   Doesn't have to be [Ramadan]. Brings you closer to God, fasting.

I see what you're thinking.

You're wondering how I could get closer to God after what I've done.

You know I hated fasting when I was a kid. Didn't get it. Why would anyone think it'd be good for you to not eat or drink … ? Even cheated sometimes.

Once when I was older, it's Ramzaan and I'm in a shop trying to buy dates and get home to break fast with my brother and this old guy's with his grandson and he's holding up the queue. First he wants a few more items, then he's lost his wallet, then he remembers something else he needs – and he doesn't speak a word of English. He's Bengali going on in his own language and the kid on the till, Pakistani kid, too embarrassed to try and communicate with the old guy and getting hot under the collar. So I storm to the front of the queue and I start yelling at the old guy and shouting at the kid on the till. I've been waiting ages, it's boiling hot and there's like a massive hole in my stomach growling for food for water for this old guy to get out of the way! I've got to get home, I'm telling them, to break fast!

Kid behind the till just gets more embarrassed, takes my money hands me the dates and I leave. Got home, too late despite my efforts, my aunt's yelling about me getting the wrong kinda dates, my brother's nowhere to be seen so I leave – still haven't eaten anything. I'm walking down the road in a rage, hungry as hell, and I see the old Bengali guy sitting on the street with his grandson. They obviously didn't get out of the shop too soon so they're breaking their fast right there in the street. The kids smiling and the old guy's feeding him a banana and an apple – they didn't have much. I see this tired old Bengali guy, in the boiling heat after a 15 hour fast sipping water patiently while his grandson eats the only thing they've got before they walk home. The kid's too young to fast – was eating chocolate in the shop but still he's munching away at the fruit – asking his gramps for more water. He sees me and … I'm ashamed – don't know why. So I look away, think I'm gonna cross over the road, keep walking. But the kid runs up and pulls me over – the old guy's telling me to sit. And he gives me a date, and a sip of water – pats me on the back, like he knows how angry and hungry I am. He offers me the fruit … Three of us sat there, on a pavement in the middle of the city sharing an apple, a banana and handful of dates. I haven't missed a fast since that day.

Thing is Len, everyone in that queue – granddad included – was fasting. All of us were hungry. Everyone was boiling. That's why I was ashamed when I saw him. I'd been fasting for years and I never thought about that – ridiculous, I know. My brother, who I rushed home for? Wasn't fasting, out with his college mates somewhere in the city centre. That was it then. I wanted to know how an old guy like that, who must have been more knackered and hungry than me when I was shouting into his face in the shop – could smile and offer me a fair share at his meal when he had every right to kick off. Sometimes you have to do things for someone else – when you know you're going to get nothing back but trouble. Just cos it's the right thing to do … It ain't just about the food and drink Len, it's about who we are, from sun-up to sundown. Who we want to be …

From

A BRIMFUL OF ASHA

by Asha and Ravi Jain

Produced by Why Not Theatre and developed at the Tarragon Theatre in Toronto, *A Brimful of Asha* received its world premiere at the Tarragon Theatre in November 2012, directed by Ravi Jain and written and performed by Asha Jain and Ravi Jain. As part of a world tour in 2015, the Why Not Theatre production of *A Brimful of Asha* received its UK premiere at Tricycle Theatre on 8 September 2015.

A Brimful of Asha is a hilarious family drama, told by a real-life mother-and-son duo, about the family's pursuit to find a suitable wife for Ravi. As mother and son sit on opposite sides of a dining room table, they share the stage to tell their version of events, interrupting, talking over and chiming in to add relevant missed-out bits of information to compete for the audience's vote and sympathy. The reason for this public courthouse is to settle the growing contention of why Asha's twenty-seven-year-old son still isn't ready to settle down and get married. Asha Jain and her husband believe that it is only right, as concerned parents who simply want the best for their child, for them to meddle in his personal life and to speed the marriage process by adopting the long-standing cultural Indian tradition of arranged marriage. However, needless to say, Ravi has opted for a more westernized approach to love and marriage, wanting to maintain control of his own life by having the freedom to fall in love with a person of his desire. But mother knows best – or at least she believes she does. So alas, the dispute continues. *A Brimful of Asha* juxtaposes the life of an Indian mother with that of her Canadian son, to explore the complexities of cross-culturalism, together with intergenerational expectations and how these issues impact on a family. This comical, complicated love story deals with themes of immigration, arranged marriage and cultural traditions.

Canadian theatre director-actor Ravi Jain was born to be an artist, singing Michael Jackson songs as a child and imitating his film idol, the Bollywood superstar Amitabh Bachchan after repeatedly watching all his movies. Now aged twenty-seven, despite his parents' hope for him to outgrow his childhood fantasies and enter the real world of corporate work and marriage, he plans to open his own theatre company. As he gets ready to embark on a trip to India to facilitate theatre workshops, his parents take this opportunity to put their meddling scheme into action by hijacking his trip. After they set up dates for Ravi with Indian girls both online and across India, not to forget arranging meetings with the girls' families, Ravi struggles to maintain a calm, respectable exterior and eventually explodes, causing a heated argument between him and his mother, making his mother cry and upsetting his father. But with tensions mounting and time running out, will this family be able to stay together to celebrate the wedding day?

Summary (extract)

Twenty-seven-year-old Canadian **Ravi Jain** has taken the trip to India to facilitate a theatre workshop with his friend **Andrew**. But his family have other ideas. After joining him on his trip, his father announces his arrangement for **Ravi** to meet a girl named **Neha** who lives in Bombay. Reluctantly **Ravi** agrees to meet **Neha**, his prospective wife, but with his father leering in the background and the pressure from his Indian family all awaiting a running commentary on how it went, it quickly becomes a painful experience.

Ravi   So I say 'Hi Neha, I'm Ravi, nice to meet you. That blur
over there is my father. So, Neha and I go out and we have like
an awkward first date. Nobody mentions marriage once. And we
end up going to this pizza place called Not Just Jazz by the Bay.
And we're sitting there having pizza and drinking a coke and
for about fifteen minutes or so, I'm thinking, 'Yeah, she's smart,
pretty, we have a lot in common. Yeah, I can do this. I can totally
see myself marrying … her!?!?' But then as I have this thought
my heart starts to palpitate, I start sweating, the room starts to
spin because there's no possible way you can ever decide to marry
someone in such a short amount of time. So I start to scrutinize
all these insignificant details about her. I'm like, oh my God she
ordered mushrooms on her pizza! I could never marry someone
who orders mushrooms on her pizza! What will that do to our
kids? So, I'm literally starting to sweat like a madman. My heart
is pounding and I'm like, 'Neha, I'm having a really good time
and all, but, you know, I'm not feeling so well, do you mind if we
call it a night?' And she's like, 'Yeah, no problem. What are you
doing tomorrow?' And I say, 'Well, my dad and I are going to do
some sightseeing, see a play. You're more than welcome to come
if you want. No pressure.' And she's like, 'Well yeah, I'm pretty
busy, but I'll text you and let you know if I'm going to make it to
see the play.' Great. We say goodnight. I go home. Go to bed. Day
two. I am awoken by the auntie that we're staying with. 'Ravi!!!!
Wake up!!!! Tell us all about the date!!!!' (*referencing a projected
photo*) That's Sujatha auntie – the auntie we're staying with – the
best alarm clock in Bombay. And I come out to the dining room
and there's my auntie, my uncle, and my dad are all sitting there
having breakfast and my auntie goes, 'So … ? How did it go?'
And before I can say anything my father cuts me off and goes,
'Ravi, please, let me. Sujatha, I met the girl. And I have to say, she
is so punctual!' And I was like, 'Yes Papa, absolutely she's very
punctual. That is absolutely the reason to marry her. Very good
observation. Thank you.' Then I say, 'Well, auntie, she's very
nice, whatever, it was fine, but I just didn't feel a spark – I just
don't think this is going to happen. So can we just leave it.' But
my dad says, 'Come on you only have one more day in Bombay
so just give it a shot! Try to see her again. Give it a shot!' So I

send Neha a text with our plan for the day and my dad and I go sightsee Bombay. It's my first time to Bombay so I'm thrilled to be experiencing the sights and smells. And while I'm doing that, I get a text from Neha that says 'Sorry, I'm busy – I can't make the play but have a great rest of your trip.' Thank god. I don't have to see her again. So my dad and I finish up our day and go home. Go to bed. Day three. Last day in Bombay. I wake up and I go into the living room and my dad goes, 'Okay, so what's the plan?' 'What are you talking about Papa?' 'You didn't meet her yesterday so today's our last day in Bombay so let's make a plan! You have to give this a real shot!' And I'm like, 'Papa, you know, she texted me and she told me that she was busy. And frankly I'm feeling pretty busy myself. I think we should just cut our losses, go home, go back to Delhi. Andrew's arriving tomorrow. I'm really looking forward to taking this trip around India. So let's just kind of end it here.' And he says, 'Oh yeah, sure, sure. Why don't you go pack your things, have a shower and then we'll plan our day.' Great. So I hop in the shower and I think, 'Wow, that was so easy! I only had to meet Neha once! That was so easy. That was … way too easy! No, no, no, that`s not how it works with my dad.' So I get out of the shower, towel off, throw on a shirt and go downstairs to the living room. My dad says, 'Okay. It's all set.' 'Sorry, uh, what's all set?' 'Oh, she lives near the airport so we're going to have dinner with her on the way there.' 'What do you mean? How did you do that?' And he says, 'don't worry. I called her.' 'No, Papa, you did what? Don't you see how she was busy? She didn't want to go. So you're my dad. She can't say no to you so if call her you are forcing something to happen that's not supposed to happen.' 'Oh stop it! You are being so dramatic!' 'No! No, Papa, listen! Like, even if were to marry this girl, that's my dad calling a girl for a date! Do you see how messed up that is?' 'Oh stop your crying. Come on let's go!' So, that night I get to go on a date at a noodle bar. And it's me, Neha … and my dad. Now I should mention here that my dad is a very good businessman. Our whole lives he's provided for our family. And he's done quite well. I mention this because in this moment, he is going for the sale. Because he knows that nobody has talked about marriage, not even mentioned it once, and he's getting nervous, saying things like this, 'Oh Neha, you are going to love Toronto. Toronto's such an amazing city! We have so many Indians there, you'll fit right in! And she could get a job on Indian TV, couldn't she Ravi? We only have to contact the right person. And you're an independent girl and you've been living on your own for so many years. Ravi's an independent boy. He's been living on his own for so many years. We thought this would be a perfect match.' Neha and I are dumbstruck. Like, all we can do is just slurp our noodles. We're like (*he mimes slurping noodles*). Because we can't actually believe that these words are coming out of my dad's mouth. It's insane! So somehow we get out of this awkward night. We say goodnight at a distance. And my dad and get into a cab on the way to the airport and he says, 'Okay, Ravi, listen. So, the ball is in your court.' And I say, 'Yes! Please! Yes Papa! I've got it right here. Go play in that court five miles away! I've got it. Thank you.' So we get on this plane and go two and a half hours back to Delhi, and I'm sitting there thinking what the hell am I going to do with this ball in my court. And as soon as we land in Delhi I go to my cousin's computer and write Neha a very long email. 'Hey Neha, it was really nice to meet you. You're a really lovely person, but we are not going to get married. Okay? I only met you as a favour to my parents. Please don't get upset. Uh, it's not you, it's me.' Enter. Send. The next morning I get a timely reply from Neha and she says, 'Thank God! You're the seventh guy I've met. Don't worry about it. One day we'll all have a good laugh about this.' Great. Again, I felt like we're on the same page. Now that morning when I read that email, Andrew has arrived from Toronto and he's hanging out with my family getting to know them, and I go upstairs with my mom and my auntie to help my mom pack, because my parents are heading back to Toronto the next afternoon. And my auntie turns to me and she goes, 'Ravi, what's the matter with you? Just get married! Get it over with! We'll have a party. We'd all be way happier if you'd just get married.' And I turn to my mom and say, 'If I were going to marry someone I would need to know them for, like, I don't know, at least six months. Six months seems like a reasonable amount of time to get to know them and choose if that's the right person to spend the rest of my life with.'

From

THE BELOVED

by Amir Nizar Zuabi

The Beloved was first produced by the Palestinian theatre company
ShiberHur in a Young Vic production co-produced with the Bush
Theatre and KVS Brussels, on 21 May 2012. This production was
directed by the author, Amir Nizar Zuabi, with the following cast:
Sivan Sasson (Wife), Jonatan Bukshpan (Young Son), Makram
J. Khoury (Abraham), Rami Heuberger (Son), Rivka Neumann
(Mother), Taher Najib (Wise Ram) and Samaa Wakeem (Young
Lamb).

Amir Nizar Zuabi rehashes the biblical story of Abraham and
Isaac to create a harrowing family drama about human sacrifice,
faith and love. The story of Abraham is well known and celebrated
in three religious denominations, namely Islam, Christianity
and Judaism, used as a significant example of faith. God tested
Abraham's devotion to him by asking for the ultimate sacrifice, his
own flesh and blood – his son. Abraham passed the test because he
was prepared to sacrifice his only son, demonstrating his complete
submission and devotion to God.

In *The Beloved*, Zuabi revolutionizes the story of Abraham by
adopting magical realism and setting the play against the backdrop
of the conflict in the Middle East. Set in a home located near the
border at time of war, destruction and atrocity, we are forced to
question the act of human sacrifice in the name of religion and
authority, as well as the psychological impact it has on the next
generation.

In Zuabi's beautifully crafted abstract story, the sacrificial lamb
is personified to form the character of Young Lamb, who not
only speaks but whose piercing high-pitched bleat replaces the
harrowing cry of the son, mother, Wise Ram (who witnesses
the attempted murder) and even God. The bleating sound is a
repetitive noise throughout the piece, allocated at the optimal
moments; it is this sound which stops Abraham from killing his
son with a knife in the mountains. Unlike the biblical versions,
the play's protagonist is Abraham's son, who, after his visit to

the mountains with his father, returns home without any obvious physical scars but is mentally damaged. The story follows his turbulent journey from a ten-year-old child post-mountain trip and then again several years later as a thirty-year-old husband, to show the lasting impacts of emotional trauma caused by witnessing his dad trying to kill him with a knife – an event which has costly consequences on the son's relationship with his parents and his wife.

The play opens with the Son and Abraham returning to their humble abode several days after their unannounced trip to the mountains, confronted by a distressed Mother. The ten-year-old Son is forbidden to speak about his experience in the mountains, which causes his mother to become even more anxious, as she proceeds to strip her son to his underpants searching for evidence of mistreatment. The reason for the Mother's erratic behaviour becomes clear when we learn about her first-born son, who under the guidance of Abraham was taken by the army and died in war – a memory that has cast a grey cloud over the marriage ever since. The couple constantly fight about their only living son. Abraham wants to toughen his son to prepare him for fighting in the war, in contrast to the Mother, who wants to preserve his innocence and keep him as far away from the war as humanly possible.

As the play develops, the Son's emotional state deteriorates rapidly; he begins to reject the lamb stew that he loved so much and has a complete mental breakdown at the dinner table. This outburst leads to the Mother and Son escaping from the house without Abraham's knowledge.

Twenty years later, the Son is now a thirty-year-old butcher happily married to his loving Wife. But things take a drastic turn when the Wife announces that she is pregnant with a boy. The Son acts out of trauma-induced rage and violently assaults his wife, claiming to be inadequate to be a father to a son and intentionally causes her to have a miscarriage. The Wife leaves and the Mother returns to care for her mentally unstable son. But seven years later the Wife returns unexpectedly to give the Son the biggest ultimatum of his life. Will the son be courageous enough to return to the Moriah mountains, the place where his life transformed forever, to take the life of his controlling father in order to regain control of his own life, repair his marriage and fulfil his wife's desire of procreating new life?

Summary (extract)

Abraham (late seventies) is on a mountaintop holding a gun pointed at his son. The **Son** leaps on him and wins possession of the gun, with which he beats **Abraham** to the ground and ties him with a rope. The **Son** then proceeds to sharpen a butcher's knife. A beaten and tied **Abraham** is forced to answer truthfully the question of why he took his son to the mountains when he was just ten years old.

Abraham   Stop, son,
I beg you …
Do you know what you're doing?
I am your father.

[…]

Remember I taught you how to eat a nut?
Chew it carefully, ten times in each side of the mouth so you don't
choke? Ten times.

[…]

I covered you in the cold nights. Remember?
I taught you not to run with your hand in your pockets.
Forgive …

[…]

Stop – I beg you, stop!
I had a vision.
I had a vision.
Your brother was always there between us.
Every time I hugged you – I smelled him,
every time I looked at what I had I remembered what I lost.
I started hating that you are so beautiful and alive.
My first son, my beloved son who was sacrificed in war,
was rotting under the grass on the mountain near the border.
Then one day a brown ram looked at me and told me,
'Put your young son in the grass and take the beloved one out.'
He told me that I heard him.
He said that your brother is waiting under the grass for me.
Under the thick green. That's what he said.
When I took you to the mountain
I wanted to put you in the grass and take him home,
that's what I wanted to do.
I had a vision – it was a sign.
When we got to the top of the mountain
it was very windy.
We sat in a patch of grass.
You put your head in my lap and fell asleep.

I took my knife out, put it on you your throat.
And then I saw –
I saw your ear.
I couldn't move.
An ear – so complex, perfect, helpless.
Everything about you was malleable and burnished.
I didn't know anything could be so warm, so alive.
The knife was ready in my hand but
your neck, your lips, your tight shut eyes and your ear
shouted:
'Wait, wait. Do not harm the boy.'
I held the knife … up …
He was right, the brown ram, he was right.
I found The beloved one.
I found you …
Your head heavy on my thigh.
How simple is human happiness.
I didn't move. My leg went numb.
I sat there like a stone.
How simple was human happiness.
I saw the lamb again, he was bleating in the wind;
I moved.
Then you woke up and saw the knife.
And there was no way back.
Forgive me.
I was full of love for you. Forgive …
You said you will forgive – forgive,
I beg you. Go back … to your wife … Go back.

From

ADRIFT

by Marcus Youssef

First produced as *Adrift on the Nile* at the LSPO Hall St John's, Newfoundland, as part of the 2006 Magnetic North Theatre Festival, co-written by Marcus Youssef and Camyar Chai. The play was then re-written by Marcus Youssef and presented by the Vancouver East Cultural Centre in February 2007. Both productions were directed by Camyar Chai. The original cast was as follows: Alek Lazaridis Ferguson (Anis), James Fagan Tait (Amm), Kathleen Duborg (Layla), James Long (Mustafa), Laura Sadiq (Saniya), Marcus Youssef (Ali), Bill Merchant (Ragab), Adrienne Wong (Sena), Maiko Bae Yamamoto (Samara) and Sam Shalabi (Musician).

Inspired by the novel *Adrift on the Nile* by Egyptian Nobel laureate Naguib Mahfouz, Youssef's provocative play adopts a similar plot outline to the book. This story begins with light comedic moments which darken as the play continues. Set on a Nile river boathouse in downtown Cairo, a group of middle-class Egyptian friends gather for the nightly parties, where they smoke hash, marijuana or water pipe of kif and talk light-heartedly about personal, racial and political grievances.

The mood rapidly changes when an attractive hijab-wearing journalist, Samara, arrives on the boat. Her beauty captures the hearts of the men, especially Ministry of Health auditor and recluse Anis, who is catapulted back to his past life in a village and reminded of a painful memory that he suppresses by over-indulging in illegal drugs and loose women. But Samara's beauty has the reverse effect on the women. Saniya is threatened by Samara's youthful beauty and fears her looks have stolen the attention of her long-standing husband, Ali. But its Samara's intelligence, activism and no-nonsense political acumen that has an unnerving effect on the entire party. Samara's words challenge the friends' inactivity on modern-day political issues, and gradually they begin to consider acts of activism.

We begin to see Anis fall further in love with Samara, and for the first time in a long while he opens up about the loss of the two great loves of his life, his wife and child who were killed in a car accident. But Anis's feeling are not reciprocated by Samara, who has fallen for the famous non-committal film star Ragab. Things get even more devastating for Anis when he finds Samara's Blackberry mobile and discovers that she has been writing an article about their experiences for a newspaper. In a rage, Anis exposes the secret unethical actions of the party guest and falls more deeply into an unhealthy state of mind. The friends force him to join them on a fun road trip (an intervention), which leads to the killing of a stranger in a hit-and-run accident. The cocktail of drugs, grief and jealousy combined with a fatal accident leave Anis, the Master of Ceremonies, alone contemplating his life and the lives of those from around the world.

Set against the backdrop of the war in Iraq and coltan mining in Democratic Republic of Congo, *Adrift* forces us to question our secularism, fundamentalism and ethics in relation to topical political issues.

Summary (extract)

This speech is extracted from the opening scene of the play. **Anis**, a thirty-year-old, pot-smoking auditor for of the Ministry of Health, talks directly to the audience about his drug use, suicidal thoughts and the whale – his imaginary companion.

Anis You ready? Good. I'm glad you are.

What do you think of when someone says Egypt, the Middle East? Pyramids and car bombs? Fanatics and burkhas? Aladdin? Born in Arizona, moved to Babylonia?

Or me. Little old me. Getting really stoned.

He tokes.

So, about three weeks ago I was at work, in the Mogamma Building, in downtown Cairo. It's so fucking ugly, this building. Sorry. Anyway, I was at my desk, doing what I usually do, watching a cockroach climb the wall, and I look up and outside my window I see this giant whale. Bit of a shock, when you're on the fourteenth floor. Then the whale floats over and starts tapping on the glass with its fin. I opened the window. What are you going to do? 'I've been watching you,' the whale tells me. 'If I were you, I'd just end it all right now. The window's open. Go on.' A whale with keen psychological insight. I was going to ask him some questions: you know, 'Do you have some kind of degree? And, what's with the flying?' But right then, my boss barges in and he's really pissed. Apparently I gave him a report on wait-list times and, well, it was blank. Guess I forgot to save. Whoops. 'How can you type out a whole thirty page report and forget to save the file?' my boss wants to know. Good question. I was going to refer to the whale, but by then it had split. ' I know exactly how,' my boss tells me. 'Because you were stoned!'

Anis *tokes.*

Aw, come on! Stoned? Me? At work? What are you talking about? I don't smoke dope, marijuana, kif. It's bad for you. It dulls your senses, blocks out the world and MAKES YOU FORGET; who would want to do that, when the icecaps are melting and there's troops on the streets and and world's going to hell in a hand basket and what are you doing? Well, twenty-eight thousand keystrokes of data entry, if you're asking me.

Seen my airbone whales lately? Could be a global phenomenon. Maybe there adapting. Maybe there's nothing left for them in the sea. Cairo. You. Me. April, month of dust and lies. The whale was right. Three weeks ago, all I really wanted was to die.

Anis *sings 'Baby Beluga'*

From

FIREWORKS (Al'ab Nariya)

by Dalia Taha

translated by Clem Naylor

Fireworks premiered at the Royal Court Jerwood Theatre Upstairs in London, in February 2015. This production was directed by Richard Twyman, with the following cast: Eden Nathenson (Lubna), Shakira Riddell-Morales (Lubna), Sirine Saba (Nahla), Shereen Martin (Samar), Yusuf Hofri (Khalil), George Karageorgis (Khalil), Saleh Bakri (Khalid) and Nabil Elouahabi (Ahmad).

Through Taha's play we realize that childhood innocence is hard to sustain when you live in war-torn Palestine. Set in Gaza City during one of the most vicious Israeli invasions in the early twenty-first century, the story focuses on two families who both struggle to shield their young children from the brutal realities that exist just outside their apartment block. With recent bombing of school shelters and the daily deafening sounds of bombs (referred to as fireworks by the parents) filling the air, the apartment block becomes their only place of safety. As the siege continues to intensify, the parents' attempts to pacify their children's fears and escape the harsh realities of war through imaginative play and fairy-tale-like stories fail miserably. One can never underestimate the high receptiveness of a child, as both Lubna and Khalil prove they are far more knowledgeable about the atrocities of war and the reason for the big bags which sit under the eyes of those who grieve. Dalia Taha's play *Fireworks* shows how war denies the strongest instinct of a parent to protect their children and inevitably the roles between parents and children switch, leading to a world where the children become parents and parents become children.

Set in a small Palestinian town, *Fireworks* tells the story of the last two remaining families to reside in the same apartment building. The protagonist is a bright twelve-year-old girl, Lubna, who lives with her mollycoddling father and her grieving mother. It's been six months since the death of her brother Ali, shot by a soldier for no reason. The play opens with Lubna casually telling her dad about the song she wrote in her head, about someone getting shot; we realize later that this is a premonition.

Both Lubna and her mother Nahla are tormented by their inability to dream of Ali for different reasons. Lubna is consumed by guilt after breaking the picture frame of her brother, which she did out of jealousy for her mother's attention and love. However, Nahla's mental stability has wavered dramatically since the loss of her son; she is unable to sleep or be intimate with her husband, Khalid, causing a rift between her and the rest of the family. When Nahla discovers that her neighbour Samar has connected with her son through her dreams, she becomes resentful and begins to crack even more. Subsequently Lubna becomes a parental figure in the household, concerned and caring for her mother.

The chaos of the war has also leaked into the neighbouring downstairs apartment of Samar and her husband Ahmad. Their kind and over-sensitive only child, twelve-year-old Khalil, has become violent, lashing out at his mother and throwing a glass in her face. His behaviour is due to his world abruptly becoming smaller – he is confined to playing in the apartment block, with power cuts preventing him from watching television, including his favourite show *Ninja Turtles*. The couple struggle to agree on parenting strategies, as Samar wants to keep her precious child as a baby but Ahmad is keen to treat him like an adult and prepare him for war.

In the confusion of their home environment, Lubna and Khalil find comfort in their new-found friendship. As the two children play on the stairwell of their apartment block, their understanding of the war, weapons and the brutal effect it has had on the community, as well as their own fears, are played out through playful improvised stories. But Lubna's expectations of her father suddenly shift when she starts her menstruation. She demands that her father treats her as a young woman, starting by telling her the truth about her mother's condition.

As Eid approaches, the parents try to convince their children that the fireworks (bombs) will end on the first day of Eid. But as the war intensifies, coming closer to their apartment block, confessions of acts of defiance against the Israelis and conflictual desires to remain in the apartment block result in both families struggling to keep alive and stay together.

Summary (extract)

Ahmad (a man in his late thirties, Samar's husband) is enjoying the closeness and banter with his wife as he washes her in the bathtub using bottled water. But **Samar** has something which is bothering her and chooses this moment to confront **Ahmad** about a conversation she overheard about him planning to blow up a restaurant to scare the Israelis.

An activist at heart, **Ahmad** is forced to tell his nervous wife the truth about his recent bomb threat activity.

Ahmad   They have to think there's a bomb. That's the whole point. They get scared, and they run away, and they get completely confused. And then they start getting scared just thinking about going out or going to a bar or going to a café, or going –

[...]

Because we don't have tanks, and we don't have weapons, and we don't have planes, and we don't have anything. The only thing we can do is make them scared.

[...]

It's just a threat. To scare them a bit. So they understand what it's like to be crammed into our houses waiting to be blown up. It's been weeks already and God knows how long it will last. They're killing us like flies. They've destroyed our city. I went up on the roof. You can't recognise it anymore … It'll never be the same again. They've ruined everything. Have you not seen what's happening? Have you seen on TV? Through the windows? Have you been able to sleep? There's nothing left of it. When was the last time you slept? When Khalil asks questions, I don't know what to say. I don't know what to tell him, what to teach him. And right now right now right now when we're dying, when they're killing us just because they can, when we're silent in front of our kids' questions, they're on top of a hill watching the planes bombing us and cheering. They're cheering. An hour away from here they're living. They're going on with their lives, they're not scared, they think they think they think they can do anything and nothing will happen to them. They're happy. They can put their children to bed and know there'll find them there in the morning. They can send their kids to school and know they won't have to come and pick them up in pieces. They think they can do whatever they want, and we'll forget. No no no no no, we won't forget. No I'm not going to forget, and you're not going to forget and Khalil won't forget, no, Khalil won't forget. You can forget for a while, yes, for a while when they're busy with life. But it'll always come back, haunt us. We can make them scared, make them terrified, make them look over their shoulders when they're out, when they're on the bus, when they're having a night out, when they're on the beach, when they're just walking about. Now just think – when I call the bar and they all get up and run about like they've lost their minds. Just think of them running out into the streets in their nice dresses and their high heels and their fancy suits, the girls with make-up running down their faces because they're scared. Then they'll remember what's happening here, what's happening an hour away. Then they'll think of us. Maybe they'll know? Maybe they'll stop? Maybe something buried deep inside of them will wake up.

From

ARCHIPELAGO

by Caridad Svich

Archipelago received its world premiere at the Ilkhom Theater
of Mark Weil in Tashkent, Uzbekistan, produced by Irina Bharat
and Tyler Polomsky for the spring 2014 Festival of American
Work. The play was translated into Russian for this production by
Oksana Aleshina and directed by the artistic director of the theatre
Boris Gafurov, with the following cast: Olga Volodina (H) and
Maxim Fadeev (B). *Archipelago* was a nominee for the Kilroys'
2014 THE LIST for Best New Plays.

Svich's writing style could be likened to the work of Debbie
Tucker Green, Sarah Kane, Samuel Beckett, a master of language
and thus a genius in engaging the audience with the nothing more
than a vague setting, choppy sentences and powerful monologues.

Archipelago is greater than a play with themes, as it is more
preoccupied with understanding humanity through an exploration
of the strength and fragility of the human mind. Rightfully
referred to as a memory play, Svich playfully focuses her play
on the act of memory, the obsession to create and revisit fond
memories, as well as the inability to control our memories as a
result of aging, trauma or dementia; a complete wipe out of an
entire lifetime of memories.

The relationship between the two characters in the play is
anchored by their shared memories, which over the course of the
play acts as both a comfort and irritation. From being lovers on a
bridge, to days of slumming through the city, squatting and living
off a diet of gummy critters and chips out of machines the couple
continue to navigate their relationship through times of austerity
and war avoiding bombs and bullets along the way.

Against these bleak times, their differences become apparent
which results in them losing each other for the first time. But as
faith would have it, years later, they are reunited.

But just as things begin to look brighter, a tragedy occurs, resulting in a coma which threatens to separate the couple for good.

Summary (extract)

After losing each other for the first time, the couple have found each other several years later. But as they slip into a place of familiarity and happiness, a gunshot leaves **B** falling to the ground and **H** left in darkness.

This monologue by **H** has been extracted from the beginning of the next scene entitled Forgetting (2nd Leaving).

B   I wanted to tell her everything about everything about armed
soldiers patrolling the streets roads cut off by wire and concrete
and bayonets fixed to barrels and brothers dead in prison and
planes overhead and the swift crack of rifles and drones and
whatever else was fit to send over sky and walls and shrubby
desert and vastness and how here in the city, her city, her streets
of angels, there were walls too just like home just like the vacant
eyes of guards who were my cousins and thieves who were my
friends and how the word terrorist was never spoken except in
signs made by hands and fingers and marks sometimes on a
page sometimes for hours when thumbs were cut off for leaking
information and hands were tied for telling truths and territories
were occupied for hundreds of years without any real hope of
peace because the lines had been drawn on historical maps and
we couldn't bring ourselves to even think past what had happened
yesterday and the day before the wandering began in these lands
of plenty made lands of possible ruin and how if you shouted the
birds mimicked the shout with such precision dead feathers fell on
the ground every day and soon the desert was a blanket of feathers
bloodied and torn and left for fresh graveyards and stone markers
along roads and flowers burnt by someone else's design and you
couldn't see past the end of the lines of the lines of the dead and
the ghosts in the air who laughed and sang and cried and beat
their drums with anguish and rage and tones of cruel indifference
to the tides of peoples trying to escape the politics of hate and
slow-moving change but if you looked real close for a split second
if you looked without blinking past the lines of scrappy trees
standing still in the midday sun you could see a child a small child
pointing a small gun at whomever stood in their way and it was
this child in his olive greens in her patched-up jumper who held
the center of the world in his her hands with a mere shot/ pop
like the sudden bump of bumper cars in the arcade by the shore
and the electric lanes near the end of all summers when we were
young and pretended that hate was a word and love was a concept
and all we had to do to get by was to drift and race and sleep and
use words like socialism and tribalism and democracy without
really considering their context because to think too much would
mean we would know ourselves too deeply and we couldn't risk

anything but dreams and possibly the word hello, and as I thought
of my fallen brothers and packs of yellow dogs littering the roads
with their rotting stench and the stinging rain of the desert heat
of my long ago childhood long ago like an old book buried in
some stone library that would one day be blown up by a wave of
car bombs to make way for a multi-story car park and the gliding
hotel of an ever-promised future I whispered in her ear the soft
panicked whisper of a child who missed and feared his home and
didn't want to know anything about the record of his life because
if it were to be played before him he would likely scream and lose
all the cool he had built up so well for so long and he would most
definitely be found out and heaven knows what kind of justice
would await him on this earth if anyone were to know in all the
history of feeling that he had never known a true sense of peace.

Forties +

From

TEN ACROBATS IN AN AMAZING LEAP OF FAITH

by Yussef El Guindi

Ten Acrobats in an Amazing Leap of Faith received its world
premiere at the Silk Road Theatre Project in Chicago in 2005. This
production was directed by Stuart Carden with the following cast:
Vincent P. Mahler (Kamal), Irit Levit (Mona), Kareem Bandealy
(Tawfiq), Anil Hurkadli (Hamza), Monica Lopez (Huwaida),
Peter Nicholas (Murad), Frank Platis (Aziz), Mary Ann de la Cruz
(Pauline), Jen Albert (H.D.) and Steven Gilpin (Kevin).

Far away from the world of terrorism, Yussef El Guindi's comical
melodrama features an ordinary Arab-American Muslim family
dealing with everyday contemporary issues. Yussef El Guindi's
inspiration to write *Ten Acrobats* came from wanting to combat
the saturated negative stereotypes that were portrayed around the
world after the 9/11 attacks, showing the humane side of the Arab
and Muslim community. That being said, this play is far from
mundane, dealing with complex themes such as homosexuality,
feminism and atheism. Guindi brilliantly strikes a balance between
drama and humour as the lead character, Kamal, the father of
the Fawzi family, struggles to accept the liberal choices of his
children. Kamal and wife Mona arrived in Los Angeles from
Egypt twenty-five years earlier, a decision that went against the
wishes of Kamal's father, but one which gave them a successful
carpet business and enabled them to offer a better life for their
children. With a life of luxury and more freedom than Kamal
ever had when he was growing up, he wants one thing from his
children – and that is for them to value family cultural traditions
and live a Quranic way of life. But it's not long before secrets
are revealed, family traditions and practices are challenged and
generational frictions threaten to tear the family apart for good.

Set in present-day Los Angeles, the play opens a day before Kamal
and Mona's only daughter Huwaida's engagement. But in the midst
of preparation, their son Tawfiq has a confession that he needs
to tell his father. Despite Mona's pleas for him to tell his father a

week after the engagement, Tawfiq cannot stomach the thought of attending Mosque with his father without bearing the news. Before leaving the house for the second time after forgetting his bag, Tawfiq comes clean by admitting he no longer wants to attend Mosque with him ever again and also no longer wants to be considered a Muslim. To make matters worse, Tawfiq has secretly arranged for his sister Huwaida to meet the man she is expected to marry for the first time since they were children, and after an awkward conversation made even more difficult due to a language barrier, she decides she wants to break off the engagement. Just when it seems things cannot get any worse, Kamal and Mona's other son Hamza is caught by the police and jailed for having sex in a public place, after he was caught with his pants down with his oud music instructor-cum-boyfriend, Kevin, during their oud lesson in the park.

Against the backdrop of society's prejudiced attitude towards what it means to be Muslim in twenty-first-century America, each character struggles to find a balance between honouring their cultural traditions and Muslim religion whilst living and fitting in at their place of residence in America. This exploration is played out during Huwaida'sscenes with psychiatrist Pauline, as she speaks about her haunting dreams of dressing in a veil and swimsuit for a beauty pageant – an image that made her feel both a sense of enjoyment and mortification.

Summary (extract)

A tense, uncomfortable atmosphere at the Fawzi residence. **Kamal**, the father of the family – born and raised in Egypt as a conservative man and devout Muslim with respect for cultural traditions and practices – has recently found out that his son **Hamza** was caught carrying out a sexual act in the bushes with another man by the police. The oud which the son was meant to be practising in the park with his instructor, now sits on the coffee table in the family living room. **Kamal** stands staring at the oud; **Mona** (his wife) sits on a chair. His son **Hamza** is also seated, staring fixedly ahead. **Hamza** is desperate to leave the living room but his father refuses to excuse him. It is all too much for **Hamza**, who stands abruptly and begins to move away. **Kamal** stops him by plucking at the oud and speaking.

Kamal Did you ever practice? (*Strumming a few strings.*) My
mother always thought it a vice of my father's playing this ... He
would come home and get drunk on this instrument ... Shut us
out with the pleasure he found in it ... Sometimes making us be
his audience. We would dutifully listen – and sometimes enjoy
– but most times ... I would grit my teeth and pray the song
was short ... He made it seem such a joy ... I envied him his
passion ... I always wondered where he went in his head when
he played.

...

Yes ... Perhaps it is best he is dead after all ... He would have
been upset that the grandson who continued his passion was
caught with a man in the bushes, and that his beautiful oud was
nearby. 'What,' he would have said, 'You couldn't have left the
oud behind. You had to drag it into your filthy habit.'

This, an inspired instrument, that calls out the best in us, this you
had to have next to you while you were debasing yourself?'

...

This will be in his record. This ... stain. This ... abomination. This
is public record. You know this is public record? For everyone to
see. This will spread like wildfire-in the community and back to
Egypt. Oh they will love this. We will be the best show in town.
We are supplying them with all the drama they need. Switch off
your televisions and come see the Fawzi family as they explode.
First my son goes insane and becomes an atheist; then, my
daughter goes insane and dumps the engagement, and now, my
other son goes insane and goes fornicating in the bushes. What
happened? Did they change the drinking water on us? Is there a
virus going 'round that is affecting our ability to be sane? Decent?
Oh. (*A short laugh.*) We did a wonderful job. You especially, my
dear, with your wonderful ability to damn your children to all the
freedom they could ever want.

...

Not enough. What's next? Suddenly I find myself in a new family with new rules and thinking. What is up next? Let it *all* happen. Bring it *all* on today.

From

A WOLF IN SNAKESKIN SHOES

OR THE GOSPEL OF TARTUFFE

by Marcus Gardley

A Wolf in Snakeskin Shoes received its world premiere at the Tricycle Theatre on 8 October 2015. This production was directed by the Artistic Director of the Tricycle Theatre, Indhu Rubasingham with the following cast: Lucian Msamati (Apostle Toof), Adjoa Andoh (Peaches), Ayesha Antoine (Africa), Michelle Bonnard (Dorita/Maxine), Sharon D. Clarke (First Lady), Wil Johnson (Organdy), Karl Queensborough (Gumper) and Angela Wynter (Mother Organdy).

Award-winning American playwright Marcus Gardley reimagines the story of Tartuffe by Molière to create a high-energy, Gospel-praising, satirical adaptation set in present-day Atlanta, Georgia. Described as a farce with music, Gardley writes a hilarious yet poignant play about hypocrisy and greed through the manipulation of a religious clergyman who exploits his power for materialistic and sexual favours.

In this modern version, the original story of the hypocritical Tartuffe and the naively obsessed Orgon are transformed into the pseudo-pious Southern preacher and occasional masseur, Archbishop Tardimus Toof (known as simply Apostle Toof) and the multi-millionaire dying man Archibald Organdy. In a bid to save his church and to pocket wealth for himself, Apostle Toof wheedles his way into Organdy's mansion, becoming their new boarder.

Organdy, a respected widower whose wealth comes from selling fast food, is so enchanted by the flamboyant Apostle Toof that it is not long before he converts into a born-again Christian and decides to change his will. Organdy's family are completely shocked by this turn of events; unlike Organdy, they are not fooled by the pious façade of Apostle Toof and plot to expose the fraudster and get rid of him for good before it's too late. In the meantime, Apostle Toof's plans to weaken the family ties in an effort to convince Organdy to sign over his fortune and deeds to the house, seem to be working.

Organdy's only son, Gumper, heir to the family riches, is revealed to be gay; his lover, Peaches is seen in the eyes of God to be unclean and untrustworthy and is therefore moved to the West Wing of the house. Organdy's estranged daughter, who has recently arrived back at the family home from travelling around Africa and has therefore changed her name to Africa, struggles to connect with her father to influence his decisions on personal matters due to her long absence.

A family dinner threatens to undo Apostle Toof's meticulously executed plan, exposing him as a wolf in snakeskin shoes. But having already obtained the deeds to the house, is it a little too late?

Summary (extract)

Archbishop Tardimus Toof (known as **Apostle Toof**) is a charmer and con artist. He has successfully manipulated the head of the Organdy household, cheating the family out of their estate house and fortune. Before he leaves the house, he is confronted by the family and his wife, who demand that he does the right thing by giving the deeds back to the rightful owners. But with the deeds to the house in his hands and his eyes fixed on a bright future, will **Apostle Toof** act in good faith or turn his back on his wife, the Organdy family and God?

Apostle Toof   Fuck the soul! This isn't the sixteenth century, no king or god is going to descend on a cloud and save the day. This is the present and I WANT MY GIFTS! I've worked too hard. Plotted. Digged, dug up. Played them. Each and everyone – I picked you up and placed you where I wanted you on the stage. Played both sides – black and white, good and evil, wise and fuck dumb. O, I was good. Sly. A wolf to the sheep and a snake to the charmer! I climbed my way up to the top and now I want my throne! I want MY PLACE! We are born in war. This world, this hateful hell that we live in is a prison for powers that be. Every continent is colonized, every peaceful tribe is either massacred or enslaved or had somebody thrust their faith upon them nearly annihilating their history, their culture. Man has raped every mind, every grand of sand, every pound of flesh has been pounded, pounced on. There is no peace. LISTEN TO ME! There is no God. He lets a man shoot nine congregants in His own house, He lets our sons be murdered in the streets by the hands of the police, we still got children hanging from trees, millions of refugees left to flee their homes, niggas and crackers still don't get along, brothers still can't find work, our children are still being bullied, hurt, starving, sold into sex trafficking, the world economy is going to hell, women still don't have a place, people can't love who they love, we have lost the war on terror on drugs and God still won't show HIS FACE!

In the distance, we hear the **Choir** *singing under the rest of his monologue.*

[**CHOIR** JUST AS I AM, WITHOUT ONE PLEA,
BUT THAT THY BLOOD WAS SHED FOR ME
AND THAT THOU BIDST ME COME TO THEE
O LAMB OF GOD, I COME, I COME.
I'M NOT THAT STRONG, MY HANDS ARE UNCLEAN
MY HEART SOMETIMES FILLS WITH SINS UNSEEN
AND YET HE BIDS, OH, HE PLEADS, BUT CAN'T
UNDERSTAND WHY HE LOVES ME, YET I COME.]

All there is is getting yours. Hear! Clawing your way to the top of the heap and killing anybody who dares to pull you down from

your nest! Religion is story. What matters in this world is how
you tell that story so that you can survive, so that you can chew
on your one measly slice of pathetic happiness. Yes. I am alive.
I'm free to worship me now. And no doubt I'm going to have
quite a fall. For I built my world around the church … around my
wife … around these hands. I am sick now. I am FILTHY … rich
now. And I LOVE IT! I will never get clean. Oh yes, I'm going
to have a long, hard fall from grace. But when I hit rock bottom
… I won't break. I'll get to my feet, dust myself off (*Biting his
teeth*) and walk boldly into a new day! Lord you hear me! THIS I
PRAY! I. AM. GOD. NOW.

From

FREE FALL

by Vinay Patel

Free Fall was produced by Poleroid Theatre and premiered at the
Pleasance Theatre, Islington in London on 14 October 2014. This
production was directed by Bethany Pitts with the following cast:
Maynard Eziashi (Roland) and Molly Roberts (Andrea).

Free Fall is a beautifully written, hard-hitting two-hander
which tackles the taboo subject of suicide. British writer Vinay
Patel writes in an empathetic, nuanced and sophisticated way
to investigate a person's right to take their own life. Patel goes
one step further to explore the responsibility of the community,
questioning if someone witnessing the act has the right to stop
them and equally if they have the right to respect their decision
and watch them go. This one-act play explores themes of loss,
mental health and guilt as both characters are faced with the
challenging task of dealing with their own emotions and the
emotions of other people.

Vinay Patel's play is set on the Queen Elizabeth II bridge in
Dartford in Kent, England, in the dead of night, a common
place for suicide attempters and the workplace of experienced
toll-machine supervisor Roland. Roland is all too familiar with
the company's protocol for jumpers, but when faced with suicide
attempter and ex-con Andrea, the rule book goes out the window
and his desire for companionship takes precedent.

These two lonely strangers are linked by the commonality of their
estranged relationship with their children and impending job loss
due to technological advancements in the workplace. Supermarket
cashier Andrea gave birth to her son in prison during a five-year
sentence. After her release, her son, who was placed in temporary
care with Andrea's mother, rejected Andrea as his mother, with
the last visit ending in him physically attacking her. Rejected by
her only child, she now faces being pushed out by her workplace
due to the introduction of self-service machines, an improvement
which threatens to put her life back to square one.

Likewise, beneath the façade of the over-confident, talkative, Taste the Difference ready-meal-eating Roland, lies a man in desperation for a relationship with his teenage son who refuses to respond to his dad's countless phone calls and voicemail messages. He, too, awaits the termination of his employment.

A delicate moment of a hug between these two lost souls marks their first human contact in years and the last ever experience of affection for strong-willed Andrea, who exits the world as she entered it, alone.

Alone in his flat, Roland contemplates his mortality and relationship with his son and two telephone conversations potentially change his life forever.

Summary (extract)

This speech takes place at the end of the play, the morning after **Andrea**'s suicide. **Roland**, forty-seven years old, from Kent, arrives at his cramped, junk-filled messy flat. The stage directions suggest that he enters swaying, a little jolly perhaps, as if after a night out. He is wearing a bulky hi-vis jacket over his suit and carries carrier bags full of items from the office. A Taste the Difference ready meal once shared with **Andrea** makes his mind wander over last night's events, instantly changing his mood. For the first time in the play, we see **Roland** take control of his life, telling his boss and his son how he truly feels, which leaves a glimmer of hope for the future.

Roland   *He stumbles and knocks his thigh into the telephone table.*

Ugh. For fuck's sake …

His jolliness dissipates. Shoving the table out of the way, he dumps the bags.

He reaches into the pockets of his coat and pulls out a ready meal. The Taste the Difference. He looks at it longingly and pops it into the microwave.

While it cooks, he wanders to the table and sits, heavily.

Exhaustion slowly begins to creep over him. He looks like he's about to bawl his eyes out.

The phone rings. He reaches back on his chair – a perilous exercise – and just about gets it without falling.

Heeey there. How's it going, boss? Oh yeah, yeah, they don't show anyone there 'cause I'm not there … What? … No, I – I never asked anyone to do that. Wouldn't of said that, that must've been … heh.

The microwaves pings.

Oh! Give us a sec, boss.

He retrieves his ready meal and dishes it up, humming a snatch of a song as he goes. The phone squawks as he does. He returns, eating as talks. He tone is casual throughout.

OK, go. No, I ain't sick, just – Uhuh. Uhuh. No … No … I … ahhh you know what, you know what, you can't sack me, you can't sack me 'cause I was quitting anyway so fuck off, do fuck off. Do. Just. Fuck. Off.

He begins to put the phone down when a thought occurs to him.

Wait wait, hold on, hold on! Sorry, sorry, there's something I've gotta ask, I've gotta …

A beat.

Are you some bloke on a computer in India? Bet the weather's well nice.

He listens to the reply.

Oh. Colchester? Unlucky.

Satisfied, he hangs up. He takes a few more bites of his meal.

He stops. He makes a decision.

He reaches back to the phone, grabs the handset and dials a number. He pulls something out of his pocket – one of the stones [The large stones belonged to Andrea to assist with her plans to commit suicide by drowning in the River Thames. In the scene prior, she decides to carry out her suicide by pocketing most of the stones and forcing Roland to accept a small handful of stones as a goodbye gift before exiting], no answer on the phone, the barely audible rabbiting of an answerphone followed by a beep.

So. It's me. Leaving a message. As requested. Not ideal but –

This is unpleasant. He fiddles with the stone. He has the briefest flit of second thoughts but he rallies with a burst.

But I mean if you won't pick up, if you ain't ever gonna pick up, I guess I'm just gonna talk to you anyways, you prick, you fucking selfish little prick!

He flings the stone across the room.

You don't get away from me that easily!

The rage subsides.

Sorry … sorry, I didn't mean that. I just –

He gives up.

Just wanted to tell you about my day.

From here on in, he wanders about, tidying the place.

I met a girl. On the bridge of all places, if you can believe that. She was about your age, I reckon. Maybe a bit older. You both got a mouth on you, so you'd approve.

We met, got chatting about this and that, I bring her back to
mine, heh … Nah, nah, it weren't like that, your old man ain't that
kinda dog. Though she did tell me that I had nice eyebrows, which is
exactly what your mum said to me the first time I took her out.

Anyway, she was laughing, I was laughing if you can believe
that, going pretty well all things considered. Even had one or
two drinks and played a bit of that game you invented with the
dominoes, bit of a party in the end actually.

But then she says she's got to be off, she's got this thing she has
to do. I beg her to stay a bit longer, but nothing doing, she really
wants to get it done, so I let her go. And on her way up she's
singing this song, from that cowboy show …

He sings, slow, clear and haunting.

Rolan' Rolan' Rolan' … Rolan' Rolan' Rolan … Rolan' Rolan'
Rolan' …

He breaks from singing.

Rawhide. It's pretty old. I don't even know if you'd know it. As
she gets to the top of the road deck she looks back to me and she
starts to wave and I pull the blinds down. This one I don't want to
see.

And I don't know why, I think I've gone a bit crazy, or maybe the
drink got to me quick but I nearly, I so nearly – all I want in the
world just then is to run up there, step out on that girder with her
and I …

He finds the stone he chucked earlier. It makes him smile.

Ade, I know if you were here now, you'd be standing by the sofa,
pointing two fingers at me with fury like you do, screaming 'You
let her go?! That was a fucking stupid thing to do, Dad!' and hey,
that might be true, but it just felt right to me. In the moment. Felt
like the best thing I'd ever done for anyone.

He walks to the window and peers down the street.

I watched the water till the sun came up. Took a while, but it's worth it. You get some wonderful sunrises climbing out of that river, all just for you.

Boy – I don't know where you are. Don't know what you're doing, don't know what you've done. You could be on top of a mountain or under the ocean, somewhere over the fucking rainbow maybe or … or even just down the road, I dunno.

But whatever you're up to, I hope you least got someone there with you, seeing you through.

He lets the handset slip. Relief. He considers the stone in his hand.

Y'know, I didn't hear a splash.

Lights down.

Publications

Roy Williams Plays: 4: Joe Guy; Category B; Sucker Punch; Baby Girl; There's Only One Wayne Matthews. Methuen Drama. ISBN: 978-1-4725-2069-2

Refugee Boy by Benjamin Zephaniah, adapted for stage by Lemn Sissay. Methuen Drama. ISBN: 978-1-4725-0645-0

Gone Too Far! by Bola Agbaje. Methuen Drama. ISBN: 978-1-4081-4130-4

Child of the Divide by Sudha Bhuchar. Methuen Drama. ISBN: 978-0-4137-7613-6

Age of Minority: Three Solo Plays by Jordan Tannahill. Playwrights Canada Press. Includes: *rihannaboi95*. ISBN: 978-1-7709-1194-9

What Fatima Did ... by Atiha Sen Gupta. Oberon Books. ISBN: 978-1-8400-2976-5

Salaam. Peace: An Anthology of Middle Eastern-American Drama edited by Holly Hill and Dina Amin: *Ten Acrobats in an Amazing Leap of Faith* by Yussef El Guindi, *9 Parts of Desire* by Heather Raffo, *Desert Sunrise* by Misha Shulman, *Browntown* by Sam Younis, *The Black Eyed* by Betty Shamieh. Theatre Communications Group. ISBN: 978-1-5593-6332-7

The North Pool by Rajiv Joseph. Soft Skull Press. ISBN: 978-1-5937-6509-5

I Am Yusuf and This Is My Brother by Amir Nizar Zuabi. Methuen Drama. ISBN: 978-1-4081-3554-9

The Keepers of Infinite Space by Omar El-Khairy. Oberon Books. ISBN: 978-1-7831-9076-8

Red Velvet by Lolita Chakrabarti. Methuen Drama. ISBN: 978-1-4725-8243-0

Moonfleece by Philip Ridley. Methuen Drama. ISBN:
978-1-4081-3055-1

Off the Endz by Bola Agbaje. Methuen Drama. ISBN:
978-1-4081-3013-1

Southbridge by Reginald Edmund. Chicago Dramaworks. ISBN:
978-0-6926-7829-9

The Elaborate Entrance of Chad Deity by Kristoffer Diaz. Samuel
French. ISBN: 978-0-5736-9967-2

True Brits by Vinay Patel. Methuen Drama. ISBN:
978-1-4725-9481-5

Snookered by Ishy Din. Methuen Drama. ISBN:
978-1-4081-7255-1

The Empire by DC Moore. Methuen Books. ISBN:
978-1-4081-3056-8

The Fever Chart: Three Visions of the Middle East by
Naomi Wallace. Theatre Communications Group. ISBN:
978-1-5593-6337-2

*The Adventures of Ali & Ali and the AXes of Evil: A Divertimento
for Warlords* by Marcus Youssef, Guillermo Verdecchia, Camyar
Chai. Talon Books, Canada. ISBN: 978-0-8892-2516-9

I Call My Brothers by Jonas Hassan Khemiri. Oberon Books.
ISBN: 978-1-7831-9484-1

*Katori Hall. Plays 1: Hoodoo Love, Saturday Night/Sunday
Morning, The Mountaintop, Hurt Village.* Methuen Drama. ISBN:
978-1-4081-4702-3

The Methuen Drama Book of Post-Black Plays edited by Harry
J. Elam Jr and Douglas A. Jones Jr: *Bulrusher* by Eisa Davis,
Good Goods by Christina Anderson, *The Shipment* by Young
Jean Lee, *Satellites* by Diana Son, … *And Jesus Moonwalks the
Mississippi* by Marcus Gardley, *Antebellum* by Robert O'Hara,
In the Continuum by Danai Gurira and Nikkole Salter and
Black Diamond by J. Nicole Brooks. Methuen Drama. ISBN:
978-1-4081-7382-4

Detroit '67 by Dominque Morisseau. Oberon Books. ISBN: 978-1-7831-9000-3

The Bombay Plays: The Matka King, Bombay Black by Anosh Irani. Playwrights Canada Press. ISBN: 978-0-8875-4560-3

Bells by Yasmin Whittaker Khan, and *Chaos* by Azma Dar. Oberon Books. ISBN: 978-1-8400-2554-5

Mustafa by Naylah Ahmed. Nick Hern Books. ISBN: 978-1-8484-2264-3

A Brimful of Asha by Asha and Ravi Jain. Playwrights Canada Press. ISBN: 978-1-7709-1107-9

The Beloved by Amir Nizar Zuabi. Methuen Drama. ISBN: 978-1-4081-7315-2

Adrift by Marcus Youssef. Talon Books, Canada. ISBN: 978-0-8892-2585-5

Fireworks by Dalia Taha. Methuen Drama. ISBN: 978-1-4742-4450-3

A Wolf in Snakeskin Shoes or The Gospel of Tartuffe by Marcus Gardley. Methuen Drama. ISBN: 978-1-4742-8089-1

Free Fall by Vinay Patel. Methuen Drama. ISBN: 978-1-4742-3422-1